EAST MEETS WEST

Volume One
Second Edition

Joan Chan

authorHOUSE®

AuthorHouse™ UK Ltd.
500 Avebury Boulevard
Central Milton Keynes, MK9 2BE
www. authorhouse. co. uk
Phone: 08001974150

First Published by Author House 12/14/2009
Second Edition Published by Author House 11/16/2013

ISBN: 978-1-4490-2127-6 (sc)
ISBN: 978-1-4670-0486-2 (e)

This book is printed on acid-free paper.

CONTENTS

Introduction iii

Preface v

Acknowledgement vii

About the Author ix

An Article in The Sunday Times to introduce
    the life of some little people xiii

A Life In The Day Of Wilfred Chan 1

Chapter 1 9

Chapter 2 18

Chapter 3 31

Chapter 4 43

Chapter 5 54

Chapter 6 66

Chapter 7 74

Chapter 8 81

Chapter 9 89

Chapter 10 108

Chapter 11 128

Chapter 12 146

Religion and I 168

My Wards and I (48 Hours in the Dark Tunnel) 178

INTRODUCTION

This book is the culmination of more than ten years of persistent hard work, not to mention the many years of reading and thought that preceded the actual writing process. There have been many obstacles to overcome but Joan's great determination has overcome them all to bring the book to fruition. She provides her readers with an insight into Chinese culture but she also shows parallels with Western literature in her own unique but effective style of writing. It is amazing that some ancient Chinese writings have modern western equivalents. It shows that we are all part of the same human family.

Most Westerners know something of Chinese culture such as Chinese cooking, Kung Fu, Chinese herbal medicine, acupuncture etc. But how many know of the richness of classical Chinese literature, some of it having been written over 5,000 years ago? How many people in the West have heard of the Dream of the Red Chamber and the Journey to the West? Chinese culture developed quite independently of Greek/Roman culture, which is the basis of modern Western society, and is a whole new dimension to explore. Joan's book allows readers to sample 50 of the best known pieces of Classical Chinese literature quickly without having to plough through pages and pages of sometimes boring detail. She provides the essentials in an entertaining way. I hope many people will take advantage of this opportunity to explore the rich imagination and astute and perceptive writings of those Chinese authors who lived so long ago.

China is growing by the day into an economic and political superpower and it is important that Westerners have the opportunity to read the literature that has influenced the Chinese mind and thought process over many centuries. Some excerpts of Joan's essays have appeared in China Eye, the newsletter of the Society for Anglo Chinese Understanding (SACU). Joan is now a member of SACU, which was founded in 1965 to promote understanding between the people of the United Kingdom and China. This book will undoubtedly help to build bridges and contribute to this understanding.

Walter Fung 27/05/08

PREFACE

This is a people's book. It is for the ordinary people of the English and Chinese speaking world to enjoy the classical Chinese literature and philosophy in very simple and beautiful English.

They are effortless to read and very easy to digest. I avoid all the dogmatic expression and laborious writings. My main purpose of writing this book is for the multitude of the ordinary people to enjoy Chinese classical literature and to approach this big issue from a very easy path to the kingdom of the wise but rather sceptical Chinese philosophy and the beautiful but sometimes rather difficult ancient Chinese classics.

My book has a total of 3000 pages (now has reduced to approx. 1000 pages) and consists of 4 volumes. It is a translation from Classical Chinese literature, 50 prose-essays and novels, to English with a side theme of the "East Meets West". These essays are presented with maps, figures, illustrations, summary, brief biography of the writer and brief comment by me. It is unique, interesting, educational, original and very entertaining.

This is a Colossal Book Project. In every essay there is a brief side theme, comparison of the two cultures - the East and the West, covering a long period of 4-5 thousand years across the world. These original classical Chinese masterpieces are mostly serious and solemn. I try to put in fresh air in my ancient essays and also with warm human touch as much as possible.

I try to promote understanding and harmony of the people of the East and West through the beauty of five thousand year of Chinese classical literature. It aims at the general public and not just the academics. I am sure teachers and students will also enjoy reading them and benefit from them.

I like people to share the works of all these most famous Chinese philosophers, essayists and novelists in simple and beautiful English. I say to my readers again that this is a people's book. In food terms, this is not a five star hotel restaurant but is Mc Donald's Restaurant serving delicious meals for the people to enjoy in every corner of the high street globally.

Here I divide it into Book 1 (Volume 1), Book 2 (Volume 2) Book3 (Volume 3) Book 4 (Volume 4) in English Version and Bilingual–Languages English / Chinese Version

I have written and rewritten my drafts over and over again. I have put in new versions and adding in new ideas all the time. I transform my work from files to floppies and then to memory sticks. Day and night, I have changed the presentation, improved the contents, fonts, restyled the format etc. Now I am quite happy and proud of my book.

ACKNOWLEDGEMENT

I am using the beautiful images from Wikipedia. It is a free encyclopaedia. I think I owe them a lot. At present I can only afford to pay them a small donation. But I promise myself, one day, I will donate to them 10% of the profit from my book. I deeply appreciate the help and most grateful from these exceptionally good helpers, Mr. Walter Fung of SACU, Mrs. Czarina Chou, Mr. Brian Morgan, Ms. Yee Min Ho, Mrs. Yaying Zheng, Mr. Richard Pang, Mrs. Kim Sung and Mrs. Lynn Leong. Last, not the least, I am blessed to have a faithful, accommodating and reliable husband, Mr. Wilfred Chan, who gives me all the support I need. We are not rich and he is disabled but he is my Rock.

Dedication

In loving memory of my father, Pang Hon Tin
and my son, Chan Po Kwan.
They both loved life passionately and
warm-heartedly.

ABOUT THE AUTHOR

Mrs. Joan Chan, a retired teacher, is a simple and happy pensioner. She was born in Hong Kong in the year 1935. She left Hong Kong in 1963 with her husband and two babies. She spent 10 years in Ireland and 10 years in Canada. At last, Liverpool 08 European Capital of Culture in UK, is her Home Town by choice.

In her teens, she spent 6 years in Maryknoll Convent School Kowloon. Out of 40 students in her class, she was the only one refused to be baptised, even though she believes in God and firmly believes God is everywhere. She spent 3 years in Hong Kong University and 3 years in Open University. In recent years, she starts learning the basic skill of the computer. It is exciteing and very useful. Most of the time, this high tech is beyond her comprehension.

In her early years, following her husband around the world, Joan is quite welcome to all these happy wanderings. She says, "I am always moving for the best. It is a very good thing to be able to see more of the world, especially if you have the great opportnity to broaden your horizon and to taste different cultures in depth. I always consider myself lucky." She is a jack of all trades. She has been a teacher, a head teacher, a baby carer, a community- worker, an editor, a reporter, a manageress, a cashier, a news broadcaster, an interpreter, a translator and a voluntary carer for disabled people.

She retired in the year 1997. Since then, she spent all her energy, her spare time and every penny of her humble pension to work on her life long project; her brain child, the book, "East Meets West." It is her dream and her mission. She aims at a global success. Proudly, she presents this magnificent book to you and she hopes you will enjoy reading it.

「東西交匯」

Year of the Ox *2009* 己丑牛年

本書出版面世了。敬謝各界關注。我這本書，是加入向全世界宣揚中華文化的行列。許多人都是在發揚中國文化。在不同的崗位上努力工作。大專學者的研究作品，是最高層的，他們是指導大學生，碩士，博士研究生等。我此書的對象讀者，主要不是學識淵博，德高望重的學者。而是全球，能閱讀中文，或英文，或中英文的一般中外老百姓。我的文章是平易簡潔，使讀者容易接受。對一般人來說是一種享受。對教師和學生，是一本很好的古典文學參考書。並是一本通俗兼顧有學術價值的書，希望有如「春風秋雨」遍散全球。人人容易消化，均可欣然接受。

此書我用中英文撰寫，編譯，共五十篇。由「盤古初開」，至清初年間的古文及小說。全部都是深入淺出。圖文並茂。略加中西文化比較及評論。這書實在範圍太廣，雖然只是皮毛，我已窮大半生的精力，去閱讀，去預備，去研究，去寫作，改寫又改寫。執筆十多年的繁瑣過程，永無休止的校對工作，不受控制的電腦，所有之經歷，極多姿多彩，廢寢忘餐，非筆墨所能形容。在有些人心目中，我這「天馬行空」之理想構思，是十分不切實際。幸有至愛親人的照顧，精神上和經濟上的支持。及不斷耐心指教的曼城 Mr. Walter Fung，才在 2008 年獲得「脫稿」。此書經過幾十次的修改，由初稿三千多頁，改為初版的 (沒有中文對照) 五百多頁。實在是無可奈何。深信遲日再版時，會用中英雙語印發。本人自問好學，但廣而不夠精，博而不夠深。如有錯漏，我是真心誠意的請各位多多指教，

AN ARTICLE IN THE SUNDAY TIMES TO INTRODUCE THE LIFE OF SOME LITTLE PEOPLE

I wrote this article for The Sunday Times Magazine many years ago. I was overwhelmed of my Nationwide Success. The success inspired me and gave me more confidence to work on a much larger project. This is a people's article and my book East Meets West is a people's book. I hope you will enjoy reading them.

A LIFE IN THE DAY OF WILFRED CHAN

The Sunday Times Magazine
Written by Joan Chan Photograph by Roger Scruton

Most Chinese who live overseas are night owls because most of them are in the catering business. But I am an early bird. I was a restaurateur for more than 10 years but I could never adjust to the late-night closing hours. Now as a sub-postmaster I am truly as happy as a lark.

I get up at six in the morning. After watching the early news on ITV I switch on my video to watch either the latest events in Hong Kong, the Chinese Opera or *Top of the Pops*. At seven I've already enjoyed a good hour of television, prepared a good breakfast and it is time to dig my good wife out of bed. She hates to go to bed and she hates to get up. She was a community worker with the local Chinese community. She resigned two years ago and now works full time with me in the Post Office. We leave the house at 7:45am. She has 45 minutes to get ready.

It is always a pleasant drive along the River Mersey from Aigburth, where we live, to Seaforth where we work. We drive past the site of the International Garden Festival—the collective effort of the people of Merseyside to change this piece of derelict wasteland into a fantasy-fun land. Next we come to Dingle and Toxteth. They are just as tranquil and serene as the Albert Docks down the road and two majestic cathedrals on the right. Every morning we pass this spot which was headline

1

news. The ugly scene of riot left no trace at all. After the Albert Dock, the traffic increases. The legendary Liver Buildings soar into sight. The thought of these graceful monster birds harnessed and tamed beside the calm flowing Mersey signifies the triumph of mankind over evil and adversity. Sunshine or snow I enjoy this part of my long drive to work the most. The rest of the Dock Road is rather gloomy.

Wilfred Chan, a sub-postmaster, talks to Joan Chan, his wife.
Photograph by Roger Scruton

Wilfred and Joan Chan left Hong Kong 23 years ago. He was a civil servant, she was a teacher. They went first to Dublin where Mr. Chan worked as a restaurateur, before moving to Liverpool. Now Mr. Chan is a sub-postmaster at Seaforth and Mrs. Chan, who gave up her job as a community worker two years ago, works with him. They have two children: Frederick, 24, and Brenda, 22.

The Post Office opens at 9 am. All these five years, I have never opened late, not even once, because I feel strongly that it is very wrong to keep the customers waiting, especially when there is always a queue outside. They are so patient and good humoured, especially on

Thursday—the pensioners' day. Of course there is the exception. Mr. Drop-a-Penny is the exception of the exceptions. He is middle-aged, slightly crippled, somewhat scruffy, always lonesome and totally mute; even our most pleasant chatty counter lady can't get a sound or a smile out of him. He comes twice a week. Every time before he leaves he drops a penny on the floor. When he disappears my wife picks up the penny and throws it into one of the charity boxes. No one would have the heart to take away the fun and satisfaction of this little ritual.

Mrs. Last-Minute is a farce. She comes twice a week, never too late, but always in the last five minutes before we close. She shouts at the top of her voice and staggers along merrily. Once, on a sober day, she explained apologetically that she can't make it earlier because between the betting shop, the pub and the Post Office, we are at the bottom of her list of priorities. No one minds her at all.

Being so near the docks, Seaforth is a typical area of high unemployment. The crime rate is also high. The cash delivery is the highlight of the day. Once the 6ft-tall security man steps into the shop we all become alert and position ourselves in the alarm zone.

The morning is always very busy. People pour in. My three counter ladies jokingly call themselves 'pay-out-machines'. They are experienced, efficient and polite. I bury myself most morning entering all the figures into columns, adding and checking and rechecking. The Post Office also accommodates a small cards and sweets business. Both close at one o'clock for lunch—a simple meal prepared by my wife in the kitchen behind the office, consisting of boiled rice, meat and vegetables. It takes me less than 10 minutes to eat and for the next 50 minutes I lie on a small folding bed to regain my strength.

Not long ago two youths attempted to jump over the shop counter to grab the cigarettes and the cash from the till. Luckily I saw them from Post Office counter and scared them away by sounding the alarm.

My job brings me into close contact with another less fortunate section of the community. They are the unemployed. Most of them come and go with self-respect. They know the Government has a duty to look after the old, the sick, the weak, the needy and the unemployed. This is a welfare state, where human rights and human dignity matter most, and I am really lucky to be able to live in it.

Wednesday and Saturday are half-days. These are our shopping days. We usually go to China Town's Tea House to have lunch and catch up on the latest gossip; we collect our Chinese newspapers and choose the latest Chinese video to take home.

Liverpool has one of the largest Chinese communities in Britain, and the oldest in Europe. Like the other overseas Chinese, we work hard during the week and go to China Town on Sundays for all sorts of social, cultural and commercial activities.

The most important regular activity in China Town is the Chinese Sunday School. Nearly all self-respecting Chinese parents consider the learning of Chinese a serious matter. After all, who wants their off-spring to grow up to be a banana—all white under a yellow skin!

In recent years, through the pioneering efforts of a young man from Taiwan, Brian Wang, Liverpool now has a purpose-built Chinese cultural palace, The Pagoda; a weekly Chinese broadcasting Program on BBC Merseyside; and a free Chinese community newspaper.

If we have visitors we will show them the two cathedrals at both ends of Hope Street, The Beatle City, the Knowsley Safari, and finish the day wining and dining at the Riverside Inn. I am determined to show visitors the best side of Liverpool. I believe that to think positive and be positive are the only ways to overcome our problems. Liverpool is a great city.

The afternoon in the Post Office is not so busy. There are four chippies and one Chinese restaurant within half a mile. Most of their staff appear after their busy lunch trade. The strong smell of salt and vinegar (fish and chips) filling the shop signals the presence of our fellow countrymen. They are a hard-working lot. Having been a restaurateur for so long I know what their lives are like and I have great sympathy for them.

Time goes by very quickly. The Post Office closes at 5:30pm and we are home before 6:30pm. Frederick, our son, is a computer supervisor and lives close by. Three times a week he comes to cook and have the evening meal with us. After a busy day, a hot meal to come home to is much appreciated. We see Brenda, our daughter, frequently. She read economics at Liverpool University and now works for Guinness at Runcorn.

We don't go out at all during the evening. After a long working day we put up our feet and enjoy a well-earned rest in peace. All housework, social calls and entertaining can wait until Wednesday and Saturday afternoons, and Sunday. We go to bed after watching News at Ten.

The Sunday Times Magazine Written by Joan Chan
Seaforth Liverpool England 11-01-1987

EAST MEETS WEST
4 Volumes In English Language
Contents
Volume 1 English Version
12 Chapters from Chapter
1 to Chapter 12

1. Mythology Pan Gu from 'a collection of the Literary Composition' Tang Dynasty, Ouyang Xun, the Imperial editor, based on the original fragments and excerpts from Han Dynasty approx. 202 BC.
2. Book of Changes (I Jing) by Fuxi King Wen Duke Zhou Approx. 5000-3000 BC 13th century BC to 711 BC
3. The Book of Odes approx. 1000 BC authors unknown
4. Chapters from Tao Te Ching Lao Tze approx 6th Century BC
5. Bamboo Strips words of Confucius 551-479 BC
6. An Excerpt from Mencius 371-275 BC
7. An Excerpt from Zhuang Tse 335-275 BC
8. An Excerpt from Sun Tzu 5th century BC
    Introduction and Excerpts of 4 Great Chinese Classical Novels
9. Journey to the West By Wu Cheng Eng Approx. 1500-1582 (Excerpts from A GREAT NOVEL # 1)
10. The Dream of the Red Chamber by Cao Xueqin Approx. 1715-1764 (Excerpts from A GREAT NOVEL # 2)
11. The Three Kingdoms by Luo Guan Zhong Approx. 1330-1400 (Excerpts from A GREAT NOVEL # 3)
12. The Water Margin by Shi Nai An Approx. 1500-16 00 (Excerpts from A GREAT NOVEL # 4)

Volume 2 English Version
12 Chapters from Chapter
13 to Chapter 24

13. Censor from Count Jon approx 6th century BC by Zuo Qiuming
14. Minister Hin's New House approx 6th century BC by Tangong
15. Duke Hin Killing His Heir approx 6th century BC by Tangong
16. Confucius Passing by Mount Tai approx 6rd century BC by Tangong
17. Duke Kneeling and Accepting Pork approx 6th century BC Zuo Qiuming
18. Peace between Song and Chu approx 6th century BC Gongyang Gong
19. The Fortune Teller by Qu Yuan 339-278 BC
20. The Episode of the Fisherman by Qu Yuan 339-278 BC
21. A Decree from Emperor Gao 1st Century BC
22. Eulogy of King Xiang Yu by Sima Qian 145-90 BC
23. Eulogy of Confucius by Si Ma Qian 145-90 BC
24. Ode of Mulan Anonymous 6th-5th century

Volume 3 English Version
12 Chapters from Chapter
25 to Chapter 36

25. Emperor Guang Wu Giving Award approx 6th century BC
26. The First Declaration of War Zhuge Liang 180-234
27. The Peach Blossom Spring Tao Yuan Ming 364-427
28. Mr Five Willows Tao Yuan Ming 364-427
29. The Decree of The Prosecution to Mo 600-665
30. The Preface of King Teng's Pavilion 650-676
31. The Spring Night Festival Li Bai 701-762
32. The Ancient Battlefield Li Hua 715-766

33. The Dragons Han Yu 768-824

34. The Wet Nurse's Epitaph Han Yu 768-824

35. Thousand Li Horse Han Yu 768-824

36. The Memorial on The Bones of The Buddha Han Yu 768-82 4

Volume 4 English Version 12 Chapters from Chapter 37 to Chapter 50

37. The Crocodiles Han Yu 768-824

38. The Fu of Ah Fong Palace Du Mu approx 695-744

39. The Humble Hut Liu Yu Xi 772-853

40. The Tree Planter Liu Zong Yuan 773-819

41. The Stream of Folly Liu Zong Yuan 773-819

42. The Old Drunkard's Pavilion Ou Yang Xiu 1007-1072

43. The Sound of Autumn Ou Yang Xiu 1007-1072

44. Love of Water Lily Zhou Duen Yee 1017-1076

45. The Red Cliff I Su Shi 1037-1101

46. The Red Cliff II Su Shi 1037-1101

47. The Ink Pond Zeng Gong1019-1083

48. Yue Fei – The Red River Lyric Yue Fei AD 1102-1145

49. On Reading of the Biography of Lord Meng Wang An Shi 1021-1086

50. The Song of Morality Wen Tian Xian 1222-1282

CHAPTER 1
PANGU – THE CREATOR (PAN KU–GU)

From 'A Collection of the Literary Compositions' Tang Dynasty
By Chief Imperial Editor Ouyang Xun 557-641 AD

氏 古 盤

Portrait of Pangu from Sancai Tuhui
Chinese Mythical Giant of the Universe
Our Pangu has a kind, heroic and handsome face

Foreword

According to ancient Chinese mythology, Pangu was the creator of mankind. Compared to the West, he is the Chinese Adam. Legend has it that he comes from an extremely large egg called the Great Monad at the beginning of the Universe. When the egg broke, a giant, Pangu, came out of it along with two basic elements, Yin and Yang. After eighteen thousand years, Pangu died and donated his body to form the world. Finally, the human beings were generated from the fleas and mites in his skin. This fantastical and philosophical myth is very popular with the Chinese people handed down throughout the centuries by word of mouth. In the 3rd- 4th century AD. it was first put into a written record by a Taoist, Xu Zeng, although some say by Ko Hung. In the Tang Dynasty, a team of scholars worked on the first encyclopaedia of China, 'A Collection of the Literary Compositions'. The Legend of Pangu is officially recognised and formally included into this great classical chronicle.

In some legends of Pangu, our first man, has been depicted as different beings. Pangu has been the dragon, the unicorn and the tortoise. The most common and popular one is a healthy and handsome looking man coming forth from an egg with two horns, two tusks, and a hairy body, holding the round Yin and Yang symbol and wearing leopard skins or leaf patches. Some later accounts show him as god and is an important focus of the traditional beliefs of Taoism. To the Taoists, he is in a state of perfect balance and is in complete control of the forces of the Yang and the Yin. The forces are represented by the black (yin) and the white (yang) halves. But the line that separates the two halves is not straight. It becomes apparent that, as part of nature, human beings are subject to these basic laws as well. Pangu bends but never breaks; he dies but does not vanish. Symbolically, Pangu represents the giant in each of us who is capable of mastering the powerful, natural forces of which we are made. I cannot think of any better outcome of his recycled body than the one he performs. What a great imagination! What a beautiful philosophy!

Original Text

The following text of Pangu is translated and edited from 'A Collection of the Literary Compositions' approx. 624 A. D. in Tang Dynasty.

In the beginning, the Universe was in a blurred and formless chaos and it was shape like a gigantic cosmic egg. Inside this egg, Pangu (Ku, Gu) came into being.

After 18,000years, the egg cracked and heaven and earth emerged The bright and clear Yang was the Sky and the dim and murky Yin was the earth. Pangu was born into it.

He went through nine changes everyday. The gods rose to heaven. The monsters remained on earth. The sky rose ten feet every day and the earth also became ten feet thicker every day. Pangu grew ten feet taller every day. With another 18,000 years, the sky became very high and the earth very thick. Pangu had become very tall.

Pangu was the first Man that lived in our universe. When he died, his body went through many changes. His breath turned into the wind, his voice became thunder, his left eye the Sun, his right eye the moon. His four limbs and the body became the mountains and lands, the blood the rivers. The veins and muscles became paths and roads; his flesh and skin turned into fields and land; hair turned into stars. Skin and tissues became grass and trees while teeth and bones became gold and rock; the marrows became pearls and jade, the sweat, the rain. Finally, as the wind blew on Pangu, the mites and the fleas in his body turned into human beings.

Summary

Pangu was an ultra gigantic giant emerged from a cosmic egg. He lived to be 18,000 years old. When he died, his whole body changed into all the natural elements and the fleas and mites in his body turned into human beings.

Brief Biography

This magnificent myth was not written by one writer nor recorded in a systematic way.

"Three Five Historic Records", the first book mentioned about Pangu, was written by Xu Zheng, a Taoist, a great scholar and a Government Official of Wu. 229-280 BC, the Three Kingdoms periods. Some said it was written by Ko Hung, 284-364 AD. who was also a Taoist.

During the Qin Dynasty, 255BC, many classical works of literature were lost, but luckily some important and beautiful fragments and excerpts were found and circulated among the Chinese scholars for more than a thousand years. Eventually, at the 'late 7th Century AD, the Tang Scholars gathered together the scattered fragments. Authorised by the first Tang Emperor Tang Gao Jo, they worked on this big project enthusiastically and thoroughly. Led by the most renowned scholar late 7th Century A. D Ouyang Xun, 557-641, this first ancient Chinese Encyclopaedia was edited, compiled and finished in three short years. Ouyang Xun was a Confucian scholar and a famous calligrapher of the early Tang Dynasty and was also the principle contributor to this Great Encyclopaedia, 'Yiwen Leiju - A Collection of the Literary Compositions'

The Imperial Readings of the Taiping Era is another massive encyclopedia compiled by a number of officers commissioned by the imperial court of the Song Dynasty with the lead editor being Li Fang from 977 to 983 during the Taiping Era. It is divided into 1,000 volumes and 55 sections, which consisted of about 4. 7 millions words (or, Chinese characters). Pangu is also mentioned in it. After the compilation, the Emperor Taizong of Song is said to have finished reading the book within a year with 3 volumes per day.

In the early Qing Dynasty (14th Century A. D.) scholar Ma Sui edited a similar fragmentary, 「A Script of Ancient Historical Narrative,」 and Pangu was recorded in these famous books. The original book written about Pangu was far earlier than the Bible. Adam is created by God. Pangu is a magnificent myth in China. The Bible is a book of faith and is the Greatest Book ever written. Pangu is a book of fantasy with the deepest philosophical value and magnificent beauty of mankind.

Brief Comment

Apart from religious dogma, the story of 'Pangu' is one of the most fascinating and magnificent Mythologies in the world. It combines religion and spiritualism, imagination and reality; natural phenomenon and Chinese cultural symbol. This ultra gigantic giant is peaceful and gentle. There is no record of violence and no bitterness. Adam in the Bible has the similar good nature as our Giant but with a rather different ending. With Eve, Adam was expelled from Paradise and ever since then men multiply and increased on earth. When Pangu died, he donated his body to beautify the world and the mites and the fleas in his skin turned into human beings. What a fantastic imagination!

The opening sentence in the Bible is, "In the beginning God created the heavens and the earth. Now the earth was formless and empty, darkness was over the surface of the deep"-(the Genesis 1) The opening sentence of Pangu (in Yiwen Leiju)is, "In the beginning, the Universe was in a blurred and formless chaos and it ----" What a coincidence!

Some giants in the West are ferocious and blood-thirsty fighters; some giants in the East are ugly and cruel; some giants in the North are cold and fierce; some giants in the South are dirty and moody! Our Pangu in the middle of the Universe is always positive and benevolent; full of wisdom and supremacy. He has a kind and handsome face and carries a healthy and mighty body, looked smart and charming. There is no more noble donor in human fantasy Records greater and more beautiful than our Pangu!

Pangu worship

Pangu is worshipped at a number of shrines in modern China. However, most if not all of these are built mainly for promoting tourism. In these shrines, Pangu is usually depicted as a cave man, long hair, half nicked, wearing leaves or leopard skins and holding the Taoists sign or symbol, Bagua.

Legend says that the first rulers of China were all immortal and descended from Pangu, but their exact ancestry is undefined. These first recorded mythological rulers were "The Three August Ones," beginning with Fuxi during the period from c. 5852 BC These god-kings or demigods used their magical powers to improve the lives of their people. and lived to a great age and ruled over a period of great peace. Some historians identified Fuxi, Huang Di and Shennong as The Three August Ones; Emperor Shaohao, Zhuanxu, Emperor Ku, Emperor Yao and Emperor Shun as the Five Emperors. Some legend has it that Pangu is Fuxi. These are the fantastic tales from our ancestors. more than 5000 years ago. How fanciful! How imaginative!."

The Dead Sea Scrolls

The Psalms Scroll with transcription.

The Psalms Scroll with transcription.

The Dead Sea scrolls consist of roughly 900 documents, including texts from the Hebrew Bible discovered between 1947 and 1956 in eleven caves, on the northwest shore of the Dead Sea. The texts are of great religious and historical significance.

A Brief Introduction of The Greatest Book - The Bible

According to the United Bible Society, December 31, 2007, translations of the Bible, full or partial, were available in a total of 2,454 languages. It is estimated that the Bible has been changed at least 1000 times, thus meaning that God changes His rules all the time depending on circumstancs. Why not! I have written and rewritten my drafts more than 20 times in this chapter. If the words of God has to change 1000 times, my 20 changes to my humble writings is just nothing.

The Bible is the greatest of all books. It is in fact a collection of sixty–six books written over the span of sixteen centuries by kings and peasants, poets and prophets. Many of the oldest Biblical verses were first written in Greek. The Old Testament with 39 books,offers the creation of God, principles from God and recount the early history of. human race. In The New Testament, with 27 books. Jesus is its central figure. The last book, Revelation in the New Testament, tells the end of this present world and of the new world with God forever.

CHAPTER 2

Book of Changes (I Jing)
By Fuxi King Wen Duke Zhau
Approx. 5000-3000BC.

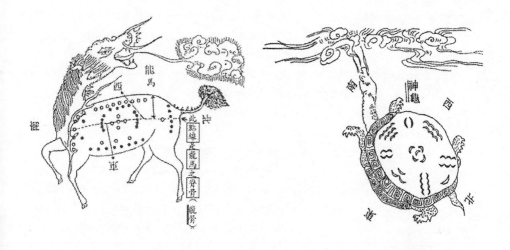

The Legendary Original Of The Book of Changes (I Jing)

River Map-at the back of the Dragon Horse Lofa Book-at the back of the Turtle

Foreword

The Book of Changes, (I Jing), is the Greatest Chinese Treasure of Wisdom, an ancient book full of mysterious and philosophical practices. Before I unfold the outer layer of this mysterious gate of divination, I write this foreword as a very short introduction to let my readers know what the Book of Changes (**I** Jing) is. I approach this subject honestly and cautiously, with great respect and feel privileged to be able to talk to you about this very complex topic, even though I can only present it at a very elementary and basic level. I introduce this great book in a simple but clear outline with some pictures and diagrams; and very brief descriptions in simple and beautiful English.

In the beginning, The Book of Changes, **I** Ching (Jing), was not exactly a book. It was the throwing of sticks and stones and scratching on bones, tree barks and tortoise- shells. Legend has it that approximately five thousand years ago, Fuxi a very brilliant chief of a primitive tribe in ancient China, living along the bank of the Yellow River, invented fire to cook, medicine to cure, tools for farming and a device to communicate with the future and the unknown. He was inspired by a Map given to him by a River Monster, The Dragon Horse. After two thousand years, his methods of divinations, have been improved by many wise men. In the year 1122 B. C of the Zhou Dynasty, this divination was glorified, beautified and improved by King Wen and the King's son Duke Zhou. As the years passed, the primitive methods of these devices had branched into different schools and developed into the most sophisticated means of learning into astrology and astronomy, fortune telling, Feng Shui practices and the philosophical Yin Yang Theory and so on. The great sages, Confucius and Lao Tze, were deeply involved with the study of these ancient wisdoms. All of these originated from Fuxi's scratched-lines and throwing of sticks and stones! Yet to the amazement of the modern scientific world, the 64 ancient symbols of the Book of Changes are written in modern day computer language. This binary system was practised by the Chinese in a similar, but very basic way, five thousand years ago. It was also predicted by the self-appointed Book of Changes experts that through their calculation of the trigrams, the year 2012 would be the end of the world. We are also told by these masterminds that the combination of our advanced scientific DNA theory may be related to the composition of the lines of The Book of Changes! Nowadays, Book of Changes has become very popular with many Chinese in their households and their lives are affected by these practices one way or the other, reasonably or superstitiously. But to the scholars and serious learned men, this is a very complex yet very interesting subject to study and to do research scientifically as well as culturally. For us lay people, there is no need to go into the area of this scholastic depth, unless you are interested in this subject and are prepared to spend time to sail into this mysterious and wondrous unknown.

A brief introduction of the basic terms of I Jing :

Yin Yang
Diagram of the Supreme Ultimate, The Taoist's Yin Yang symbol

1. Yin Yang 2. Bagua - Trigram 3. Hexagram
To the Taoist, Yin Yang is the symbol of the origin of the Universe. These are the symbols of the philosophical concepts in ancient China. The Taoist's Yin Yang symbol represents two forces in the universal. Yin is gentle and weak, the female and the moon, the water and the dim dark night etc. Yang is strong and tough; the male and the sun; the fire and the bright daylight etc.

2. The bagua is a fundamental philosophical concept in ancient China. It is an octagonal diagram with one trigram on each side. The concept of *bagua* is applied to Chinese Taoist thought and the Book of Changes, but is also used in Chinese folk culture, such as Feng Shui, martial arts etc. They are powerful source of wisdom, self judgement and determination of ones will power; and guidance for direction. The Taiji which describes by Fuxi, produces two forms, named yin and yang.
The two forms produce four phenomena, (Heaven + Earth + The Sun+ The Moon)
The four phenomena act on the eight trigrams (ba gua), eight x eights are sixty-four hexagrams. (8 x 8 x 64 = 4096)

There are 4096 (64x64) combinations and-explanations of trigrams. This is the basic introduction of Book of Changes which provides inspiration and unlimited knowledge for the majority especially for the uncertainty and unhappy people. Some successful business men, people in the stock market, politicians, and world leaders consult Book of Change in the form of Feng Shui etc. This is our Chinese way of fortune telling. We do not use crystal–ball nor have tarot –cards but we have Yin Yang and Bagua as our significant trade mark of fortune teller.

3. The text of the I Ching describes each of the 64 hexagrams, and later scholars added commentaries and analyses of each one. These have been submitted into the text comprising the I Ching. The classical hexagram sequence is also known as the The King Wen sequence. It is a series of sixty-four binary figures (hexagrams), a combination of 6 lines, either whole or broken and stacked one on top of the other. The 64 hexagrams are grouped into 32 pairs. 64 hexagrams × the 6 lines of a single hexagram = 384, the same number of days as found in ancient annual lunar calendars. The 64 hexagrams cover all human conditions, relationships and occasions, plus predictions of all kind of natural phenomenon. Legend has it, that it was first invented by Fuxi and that present arrangement and commentaries were improved by King Wen and his son Duke Zhou. Confucius added more commentaries (Judgements) and named these practices The Book of Changes. Lao Tze believed the force that depicted Yin Yen theory and thus followed the Way of Changes and wrote his Tao Te Ching.

To interpret and convince his clients through Book of Changes, the true professional diviner has to be full of confident, very knowledgeable of the reading of the trigrams and hexagrams. With a good combination of attractive display in attire, decor, charming speech and dramatic performances, most of the diviner could successfully convince his clients even in our modern computing age. The most popular practice to the Chinese clients is the Feng Shui consultation.

The following commentaries are the most useful 'Dragon Explanation' in Book of Changes. To me, it is the best section of the Book of Changes.

To some people, these lines in the Book of Changes are the most important, easiest to understand and very interesting. This is the only section, I can fully understand during my long years of reading this Great Book. The simple philosophical meaning is so plain and clear that even when I was a young child, I could remember those lines by heart. It is so easy and simple. I like the first line and the last line most. I always consider myself a little dragon, lying low and easy but always fancy that one day I am a wandering dragon flying everywhere and soaring high and free. 55 years ago, out of great surprise in Hong Kong University, Professor Liu Chuen Yan gave us a very good lecture about this Heaven Hexagram. Ever since that day, he became my favourite professor. What a wonderful inspiration 'The Dragon Explanation' has provided us.

The following commentaries are the most interesting 'Dragon Explanation', using Dragon to symbolise the move with commentaries or judgements. They provide the very wise and most sensible guide lines for us to lead a simple and happy life.

The Dragon Explanation of the Six Lines of The Heaven Hexagram

Roaming here and there   Leaping up and down   Might fall

Lying low and deep   Getting active   Soaring and flying high

In the Lowest Nine, (the first line), the Dragon lying deep in the water. It is hibernating and hiding low. It is time for resting and saving your energy for future activities. Be humble and quiet. Reserve your power and knowledge for the right moment.

In the Second Nine (the second line), the Dragon appears and comes out from hiding, roaming in the fields. The situation has improved to its favour. Seeking and looking around for opportunities, it is time to prepare and go foreword to meet worthy and great people.

In the Third Nine (the third line), the Dragon, (the worthy gentleman) is active and working hard during day time. At night time, he has to be extra careful and make sure he is safe and unmistakably in all his performance. Day and night, he has to be aware of the difficult circumstances.

In the Fourth Nine (the fourth line), the Dragon, (the worthy gentleman) is leaping up and down in the deep ravine energetically. He is performing with caution and care; make sure there will be no mistake. He is well prepared to strike and with great confidence to proceed.

In the Fifth Nine (the fifth line), the Dragon soaring up in the sky and flying high on its wings. Now is the time to advance with full force and to display your creative power. It is also time to meet some great people. The creative force is on your side. Be resolute and spread your wings.

In the Sixth Nine (the top line), the arrogant Dragon reaches the extreme height, far exceeding the proper limits. It is time to withdraw, to climb down from the climax. There is cause for sorrow if you keep on pushing and pressing. Be prepared for repentance other wise you are heading for a miserable down fall.

Brief Biography of the Five Great Sages related to Book of Changes in Ancient China:

Fuxi is one of the Three August Ones, a legendary Chief, in the Chinese prehistoric and Mythical Age. In later days, over praised by the scholars and historians, they bestow on him the grand title known as

Emperor Fuxi. In fact, he is supposed to exist at the late Stone Age of China and is just a legendary tribal chief. To say he is a brilliant, wise and a Half Mythical Figure would be more like it. He is supposed to be morally perfect, teaching his tribesmen to use fire to cook, to farm, to fish, to trap, to heal illness, to institute marriages and to write etc. In those primitive age, writing means to draw lines, to form simple figures and put scratches in tree barks, bones and shells. He is said to be the inventor of the trigrams, inspired by a Map delivered to him by a River Monster, a Dragon Horse. After thousands of years and improvement by countless wise men, it becomes a wealth of information, philosophical divination and psychological and spiritual speculation ; the everlasting treasure of Chinese Culture.

Duke of Zhou

King Wen and Duke of Zhou – The Duke is the son of King Wen, the Zhou Dynasty. (c1122-249 BC) They both contributed a great lot in arranging the Linear in order and thus create the fundamental shape and form of the Trigrams and the Hexagrams. In Chinese, Ba

Gua, the word trigram means Eight Houses. It multiples and arrives at a total of (8x8), 64 and (64x64) 4096. King Zhou and Son did most of the arrangements, combination and wrote the commentaries. In modern time, we still use most of the arrangements and commentaries presented by them. King Wen is the founder of Zhou Dynasty and he is the first King of Zhou. Before he became King, he was imprisoned by his enemy. It was during the time of his imprisonment, he started to study The Book of Changes and worked hard to rearrange the linear and complete the images and commentaries. Later his son, Duke Zhou worked with him together and thus completed the great Cyclic Trigrams and the Sixty-Four Hexagrams.

Confucius and Lao Tze- (5th and 6th century BC) They both are sages and also both have involved themselves closely with the promotion of Book of Changes to the Chinese people. Confucius included the Book of Changes into one of The Five Classics. These Classic Books were appointed by the Ministry of Education as their major curriculum for the Chinese scholars to sit for their public examinations. To be able to pass the three level of Examinations, Distract, Provincial and Court, it is essential for all the scholars to study these Classics thoroughly. Lao Tze cherishes The Book of Changes and based his thoughts on this ancient book to write his Tao Te Ching, the Taoist's Holy Bible!

Comment

I have written and translated over hundred of essays, 'The Book of Changes' is the most interesting and difficult one to translate. It is so abstract, so imaginative, so wisely written, so ambiguous and yet so valuable and exciting to know. No wonder our famous sage Confucius said, "At the age of 50, if only I have a few more years to study 'The Book of Changes', then, I should be able to make no big mistakes in my life." Lao Tze did not say much! He cherished the philosophical thought of I in his Tao Te Ching. He simply disappeared but he left his Tao Te Ching behind and influenced nearly all the scholars in ancient China to study his WAY! The laymen are too busy to study these lines. They have to work for a living. They read no Tao Te Ching nor Book of Changes but their lives are more or less influenced or controlled by the Divine Practices of the Book of Changes. Through the medium, such as the Taoist temples, Taoist priests, fortune telling, Feng Shui, traditional folk tales and the holy almanac etc., Chinese way of life completely flourishes under the Taoist Culture. I was brought up in a 20th Century family. My father was a head-teacher and my mother a midwife. In our house, we had a small family altar and a Holy Book, the almanac, to check the lucky days and hours and to consult the hidden force for big decision making. My husband is a Christian and we married in Church. But the Big Day has to be consulted with the Holy Book (almanac) first by my mother-in-law. It sounds nonsense! This is the power of our Chinese tradition and culture. This is how it affects the average little people like us! I have no time to go into the study of the involvement of its binary system with the computer and the combination of the composition of DNA in the medical science. Some self-appointed master minds even predict the end of the World is 2012 from the reading of the Book of Changes! This is very daring and scarely. I hope it is just some irresponsible prediction, wrong calculation or just some practical jokes. Let us wait and see! After all, it is only five years to wait!

Summary

The Book of Change is an ancient Chinese book of divination which is full of wisdom, predictions and guidance. It is abstract and philosophical, a collective research of sages over 5000 years. The basic writings are lines and commentaries. It includes 64 hexagrams which is built from 8x8 trigrams. Each trigram contains 3 bars or lines. These lines are either whole lines or broken ones. They stack one on top of the other. Number One hexagram uses dragon to guide you through your problems.

About Book of Changes and its Mystical Origin

In the beautiful and mystical fable of 'The Origin of I Jing (Book of Changes)' a heaven–map, namely Ba Gu, was delivered to Fuxi, a wise and heroic tribal chief by a River Monster, a Dragon Horse, approx 5000years ago. 800 years later, in the River Lo, Dayu, a great legend King, found a five colour turtle with the Lofa Book at its back This is the origin of Book of Changes (I Ching) As time went by,it developed into a book of great wisdom, deep and mysterious, the oldest form of divination, originate in ancient China, approx. 5000 years ago. It was invented by Fuxi and he first performed these devices for divination with the scratches on bones and shells using binary symbols. After 3000 years of the collective effort and improvement of our ancestors, this primitive philosophical divination was more or less monopolised and implemented mainly by the royal household. In the year 1150B. C, two great royal sages, King Wen and his son, Duke of Zhau, followed the rituals and omen, rearranged the shape and form of the Linear-Diagrams, improved the arrangements and explanations of The Book of Changes. Even Kings have to follow the Mandate of Heaven demonstrated in the Book of Changes; they have to rule their kingdom wisely and accordingly. In the 5th Century B. C. Confucius added the commentaries and included this Great Book of Changes as one of his Five Holy Classics. Now it has improved into to-days' sophisticated presentation and becomes a kind of inspiration for interpreting events to all classes of people.

The HolyBible

The Holy Bible is divided into 1. Old Testament 2. New Testament 1. Hebrew Bible, the old Testament, with 46 books, comprises three parts: "Five Books of Moses", the Prophets, and the Writings. It was primarily written in Hebrew 2. At first the Christian Bible, includes the twenty-seven books of the New Testament which was written in Greek.

The Codex Gigas Devil's Bible

Codex is the largest medieval Bible in the world and was created in the early 13th century in the Benedictine monastery of Podlažice in Bohemia, and is now preserved at the National Library of Sweden in Stockholm.

The Authors of the Bible are a collection of men and possibly women who have authored or co-authored literature. That has appeared in the various canons of Judaism and of Christianity. As of March 2008, translations of the full Bible are available for 438 languages. Portions of the text exist in 848 additional languages plus the partial 1168 or full translations of the Bible exist in a total of (438+1168+848) 2,454 languages.

Over the years, I have a habit of giving Bibles as gifts to lost souls and new born babies. I used to get bilingual E/C languages, ones with very bright and colourful pictures for their parents to read to them as bedtime stories. I always remember the saying, "The hand that rocks the cradle rules the world". It is such a magnificent book. It is out of stock now. I have sent in an order 10 months ago and they still keep me waiting. I am still waiting patiently!

I am not a Christian but I believe in God and I believe God is everywhere and is written in every page of the Bible. Christianity is the State Religion in England. Most people get baptised, married and buried in Church. The Bible is a sign of witness, righteousness and holiness of God in these holy performance. Chinese Religion is 'three in one'; Confuciusim-Confucius, Taoism-Lao Tze and Buddhism-Buddha. But none of them are God. They are great philosophers and prophets only. To me, the Bible is the only greatest book on earth with God in all the chapters. The Bible is also the only book that claims, "I am the Lord Thy God!"

Chapter 3

Book of Odes-Shi Jing A collection of 305 ancient poems (13ᵗʰ century BC-711BC) Translated and edited 6 poems from this collection

Emperor Kangxi of Qing Dynasty (Reign 1661-1722)
His Majesty is a keen patron of Chinese Poetry and Dictionary

Foreword

During the Golden Age in Ancient China, Zhou Dynasty (1122-249 B. C.) it was said that the cultured King Zhou Men Wang sent his messengers out to the four corners of his kingdom to collect many poems and songs from his subjects and then he ordered his ministers of music to set the poetry to music. Thus from the feedback he kept himself informed of what was going on in his kingdom, and knew the feelings of his people. Hence, culturally, one can say he started Chinese Literature. Politically he was considered by Confucius to be the greatest king and ruler in ancient China.

The collection of the Book of Odes, derived from a collection of about 3000 pieces of poetry covering a vast area of fifteen districts, (the seven provinces) situated along the Yellow River. It spans a period of approximately 600 years. In the Spring and Autumn Period, (722-481 B. C.) Confucius with his disciples selected, compiled and edited this great Collection into an anthology of 305 poems. Ever since, the Book of Odes is divided into four sections: (4 categories)

1. Guo Feng (Lessons or folk songs from States:) Folk Songs from ordinary people: out of 160 Songs, Odes, 60 are love songs.
2. Shao and the South, 3. Bei, 4. Yong, 5. Wei, 6. Wang, 7. Zheng, 8. Qi, 9. Wei, 10. Tang, 11. Qin, 12. Chen, 13. Kuai, 14. Cao, 15. Bin, (These 15 names are the ancient States and means folk songs)
3. Xia Yai (Minor Odes) - 80 refined songs mostly concerning the life of the nobility
4. Da Ya: (Major Odes) 31 songs of praise of their rulers and their life.
5. Jung 40 Odes (solemn hymns with music) written for religious ceremony for the court, the temple and the altar, all praising Heaven and Kings: 31 Odes from Zhou Dynasty 4 Odes from Lu Dynasty,5 Odes from Sheng Dynasty.

(The above 300-306 hand picked poems of the Book of Odes was edited by Confucius and his team of disciples from more than 3000 songs.)

Brief introduction of The Fish Hawks (The Love Birds):

I choose a few poems,(songs), from each section. This is the Number 1 of the 305 poems I choose. This song is a simple beauty. People love it, they sing it, they learn it by heart and they often quote it. They find joy and emotional tenderness in the song and it has deeply captured people's imagination. The true sentiment of to love and being loved is fully displayed in a few stanzas of this short poem. Confucius and his team of disciples chose it as the first of the 305 poems. Most probably they intentionally present a sweet and affectionate start, the beautiful side of human nature to win over the favour of the readers and the listeners. It warmly describes the sweet and true feeling and yearning of love from young people. With its artistic value forever glowing, I gladly introduce it to you for your appreciation.

Kuan Kuan The Fish Hawks (The Love Birds) Cry

First poem of the 160 Folk Songs from the The South of Zhou Dynasty. 12th century BC

Kuan! Kuan! The love birds cry on the islet in the river.
A fair and sweet maid meets a young gentleman who falls
    for her.

The duckweeds grow long and short; and drift to the left
    and to the right.
He yearns of her, anxiously thinking how to woo her in his
    sleepless nights.

After a fruitless wooing, he dreams of her all night long.
Restlessly, tossing and turning in bed, he moans and sighs.

Picking the long and short duckweeds here and there,
At last the sweet and fair maid befriends her intended in
    harmony.

Gathering the long and short duckweeds on their left and
    on their right.
To please the fair and sweet maid with bells and drums he
    plays.

The Odes of Wei 27B. C. - 21B. C.
Brief Introduction of The Big Rat:

This Ode of Wei obviously came from the hardworking peasant class. They toiled from morn till night and yet their grains and fruits of labour were taken from them by either the heartless landlord or the corrupt officials of the king. They moaned, they protested, they cried out loud and they reprimanded them. Sarcastically they condemned them, called them the Big Rats. They are angry but not in despair. Optimistically they were dreaming with hope and joy of a bright future. They sang happily that they were moving to a Happy Promised Land soon. What a positive way to voice out the loud social injustice! What a clever way to humour the greedy master! This is the virtue of the ancient peasants in China. They believe in peaceful protest. Escapism and hope for a better tomorrow to give them courage and to challenge fate and thus these brave peasants peacefully and optimistically plan for a bright and happy future, leaving their three years of misery behind. Our ancestors 'great virtue still flows in our blood. On the whole, we Chinese are proud, but meek and humble. I picked this poem because it shows the peasants' grievances but they do not turn to drastic terrorism. They are proud; they are meek; they are humble and they immigrate, escape, to their Happy Dreamland.

The Big Rat

Big Rat! Big Rat!
Eat not my millet!

Three long years! I agonizingly and unwillingly suffer from you.
But you care not of our welfare whatsoever.

We have had enough of you and we are leaving soon !
To go somewhere nice, a promised land and happy land too

Promising Happy land! Promising Happy Land!
We shall enjoy and feel free to do what we like.

Big Rat! Big Rat!
Eat not my wheat!

Three log years, I agonisingly and unwillingly suffered from you.
You have never treat us kindly nor showed any regard for us.

We have enough of you and we are leaving you soon
To a promising land and a happy land too!

Promising Happy Land! Promising Happy Land!
We shall enjoy our fruit of labour and reap what we sow.

Big Rat! Big Rat!
Eat not my new shoot!

Three long years, I suffered agonisingly from you.
I toil backbreaking day after day but you care not our exertion.

We have enough of you and we are leaving you now.
We are going to a better place.

Happy and Promising Place! Happy and Promising Place!
Who can tell that our trouble and moaning will be gone forever.

Minor Odes of the States (Feasting Entertaining Praising)

The following four Songs from Minor Odes, Major Odes, and Odes of Zhou

The four songs below obviously come from the noble house or from the royal courts and temples. All these songs praise the happy good life of the privileged and ruling classes. No. 1 song is feasting with friends harmoniously with good wine and great musicNo. 2 song is building a grand project, The Sacred Tower with the full support of his Majesty's people. No. 3. song is hailing his Majesty as he was leading his loyal peasant to plough the land and No. 4 song pictures a grand laureate to thank heaven for a good harvest.

Lu Ming - The Cry of the Deer

Yu! Yu! Happily cry the deer;
Grazing on the wild bamboo and stalking free.

I am entertaining my admirable guests;
With lutes strike and organs blow'

Enjoying the pleasant music my guest are having a good time;.
Baskets of gifts are giving out to guests as we dine and wine.

My guests like me and offer me advice good.
They show me the best way to follow Zhou's Rule.

Yu! Yu! The happy deer call
Grazing freely on the wild moor.

I am entertaining my admirable guests.
They are renowned for their virtue and brilliant righteousness.

They treat their people well, generous and kind.
A good example for the honourable man to follow.

I have good wine.
 I offer my admirable guests to enjoy.

Yu! Yu! Cry the deer happily!
They are feeding on the green shoots freely.

I am entertaining my guest-noble;
With lutes strike and organs blow'

With lutes strike and organs play
We are having a harmonious and gleeful day.

I have plenty fragrant good wine in store,
I entertain my admirable guest to drink to their heart's content.

Major Odes of the States Temples and Altars. Holy Tower Ling Tai

In the beginning, when the King builds the Holy Tower,
He plans and works on it enthusiastically with great effort and power
With the people eager to offer help around,
He finishes the project in no time.

Right from the start, they are told, no rush and no hurry.
The people simply turn up to help out voluntarily.

When the King arrives in the Holy Park,
The deer and doe basking around him.

The deer and doe are looking pretty and healthy.
The white birds look smooth and shinny.

When the king appears at the Holy Pond,
It is a lovely sight to watch the rich stock of fishes leaping all around.

Putting up stands here and there for the musical instruments,
They hang on those big gongs and huge drums to play loud and clear.

Nice music play on the drums and pleasant sounds come from the bells.
They perform harmonious music at the King's Grand Ceremonial Hall.

Accompanying by the Lizard-skin drum, as the music plays on,
The blind musicians, in front of the King, energetically perform.

Sacrificial Odes of Zhou
(31 Hymns of the Temple and the Altar)
Yi Xi

Hail to my King Cheng!
We pray with awe and thanks to God of your arrival.
You direct and lead a team of farmers,
Sowing hundred different grains.

Starting to farm on their private land,
First finish working on their thirty acres.
Then they follow you faithfully to plough your land.
Ten thousand men lead by you working in pairs, two by two.

Good Harvest (Thanksgiving
to God for a good harvest)

Good Harvest Year! Abundant with much of millet and much of rice.

The huge Granaries are full of grains stocking with billions of surplus high.

It is time to make strong wine and to make sweet spirits, offering to our ancestors.

With reverence we follow the hundred rites to pray for blessings from God.

Brief Comment

During the Qin Dynasty, it was said that (221-201 B. C.) the Book of Odes was banned and some of it was destroyed by fire. Fortunately most of the text survived orally and some manuscripts were found in hidden places. In the Han Dynasty,(202B. C. -207B. C.) The Book was restored and reconstructed back to **its** former glory. Later Book of Odes was glorified by the Confucians and was included in the official curriculum of the 'three level public examinations', the Regional, the Provincial and the Imperial. The book of Odes is not just one of the best classics in Chinese literature but it is also one of the best in the Global Ancient World Literature. Compare to the contemporary Great Works: 1. Great Epic Odyssey and the Iliad of the Greek Homer, 8th Century BC: 2. The Japanese Man'yōshū anthology, compiled by the poet Otomo no Yakamochi: 3. Regveda, the Holy Hymns of India, approx. 12 Century BC 4. Psalm of the Old Testament, to some people, our Book of Odes is the best next to the Bible. It is shorter than the Greek Epics but covers a far longer span of time and involve many more people of all classes, not just the god-like warriors and heroes or gods. It does not stop at the laborious religious rituals in their grandeur-temples and the adventures of warriors and their sacramental pilgrimage. The Book of Odes offers an insight of the solemn ceremony of temples and royal court in the formal ritual hymns and in their glorious extravaganzas as well as the humble existence of the peasants, home sick soldiers, working class and the sorrowful slaves. The Book depicts one hundred kinds of trees and plants, ninety kinds of animals and insects, thirty kinds of crops and birds and a hundred kinds of buildings, food, clothing, musical instruments, weapons, furniture and utensils etc. Thus in addition to its literary significance, The Book of Odes is an excellent document for scholars to seek an insight into the great ancient civilization of the East. The Odes includes romantic love songs of the young people; the wretchedness of the life of the humble peasant; the events of the brave and merciful warriors; the luxurious pleasure-seeking of the nobles kings and aristocrats; the colourful, lavishing and yet solemn ceremonial worship of the sacred temple and grand altars; the lamenting and sarcastic expression of peasants protesting at the injustice. It is so carefully selected there is no cruelty, no evil scheming, no violent slaughter, no treacherous murderers, no brutality and no bloodshed scenes. It is just as pure as the white clouds sailing in the blue sky, reflecting the joy, the dismay, the hope, the despair, moaning of hardship and toiling in life, the genuine feelings of fear and hope, the pageantry of the religious activities and the reality of the different spectrum of the ancient society. In short they are straight forward, natural, positive and reflect the sunny side, little rainy side of the social phenomenon of those ancient days.

The Great Teacher, Confucius, summaries the Book of Odes in two sentences.

(1) "There is no evil in the Book of Odes."
(2) "Without knowing the Book of Odes, your speech has no substance."

Homer of Greece

From the West 9 to 10 Century BC Idealized portrayal of Homer dating to the Hellenistic period. British Museum.

Homer is an ancient Greek epic poet, the author of the epic poems the *Iliad* and the *Odyssey*. He is considered a legendary figure rather than a historical person. The *Iliad* and the *Odyssey* are considered by most scholars to be the products of a centuries-long tradition of orally composed poetry. According to some, they are the product of the same poet, but for others, they were composed by different poets. Due to the contradictory, diverse and legendary or semi-legendary character of these accounts, they give no solid evidence on which to base a theory of Homer's identity. A number of traditions hold that he was blind and that he was born on the island of Chios, at Smyrna.

Some say that Homer is the moon shining brightly in the sky and the Book of Odes includes hundreds of twinkling stars, is beaming in the cosmos.

CHAPTER 4

The Canon of Virtue
Tao Te Jing 604 BC-521 BC
6 out of 81 Chapters
By Lao Tze

The First and the Greatest Philosopher of China

Foreword

Lao Tze was the first great philosopher in Chinese cultural history. To me, he is always serious and mysterious, a profound learned recluse and to most people he is the Supreme Lord of the Taoist Religion. The Taoists claim Lao Tze as their religious founder and place him in the high altar of their Taoist Temple.

Confuciusim was promoted by the Imperial Court and became the religion of the elite-ruling class of China. It represents power, authority, and righteous virtue over two thousand years in our Chinese society. Taoism is promoted by the Taoists high priests, the self-imposed disciples of Lao Tze. For thousand years these clever high priests created a fantasy playground for all ages and all classes to worship Lao Tze as their god along side with numerous immortals, ghosts and sacred animals, such as the Monkey and the Dragon. These magical practices, the concocted elixir, fortune telling, Feng Shui and faith healing penetrated and dominated part of the life of the Chinese from kings to layman, rich to poor; scholars to ignorance and through out history even in the 21st century. As you read along, you will find that many famous intellectuals and top ranking Chinese scholars were subjected to the Taoists practices. The best of the Chinese art, paintings and literature imbued the Taoists spirit.

When I was five years old, just recovered from a serious high fever, my mother told me, "The Monkey King is your newly adopted god-father. He saved your life and from now on he will protect you. You must try to be a good girl and pay respect to him especially on his birthday celebration." As any typical five years old, I was glad to have a such famous godfather and also looked forward to enjoy all the fancy offerings (delicious foods) and interesting ceremony, burning of incense etc on his birthday celebration. I was totally happy to be in this childish world of wonder and imagination. My mother was a mid-wife and married with five children with a good home. Her scientific training did not keep her away from these fancy, superstitious, ridiculous, traditional, childishly imaginative Taoist –style worship. Most of us, regardless of age, is a playful Taoist at heart. Deep inside us, there is a happy wanderer, a beautiful fairy and a romantic artist. Lao Tze is a righteous scholar, a romantic traveller, a tough old pessimist and an atheist. He left his philosophical writing behind not as a sorcerer's handbook. Taoist temples are well known for their theatrical display. Lao Tze, the recluse, would never dream of people using his name and turned him into a showy sage and a supreme lord, almost the almighty.

Nevertheless, this is part of our precious Chinese culture with a positive priceless value. We thank Lao Tze wholeheartedly because for thousands of year, he has provided a soothing and benumbing morphine. It relieves Chinese headaches and heartaches. This is definitely one of the best philosophical texts we Chinese can contribute to people all over the world to share and to enjoy. It is short and sweet. It captures the imagination of the global literary world. It is abstract and poetic, so it is easy to translate because you can interpret it in whatever way you like to suit your moral sensibility. No wonder Tao Te Jing is the world's most translated classic next to the Bible in China! Over 2,500 years, his strong ethic was the father of the none-aggressive approach to life. It helped to mould a tolerant and peaceful Chinese society. We are influenced not to conquer but to win. If Lao Tze lived in to-day's society, I think he would be given the award of the Nobel Prize of Peace.

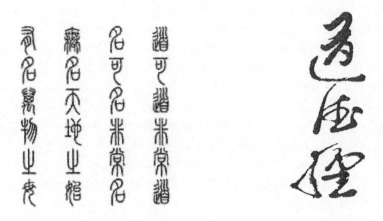

Beginning of the Tao Te Ching"Tao Te Ching", Calligraphy in Chinese seal script by Gia-Fu Feng (1919-1985)

Six chapters in Tao Te Ching:

Chapter1

The Tao that can be discussed about is not the eternal Tao;

All of the things that can be named in this world are not real things;

The Tao of the Universe comes from nothing; with no beginning and no ending.

The Universe, the Mother of the World, gives birth and names to all things. To follow the Nothingness of Tao, we possess the wonder of all things around us;

Anticipating the marvellous worldly experiences, we follow its magic-path.

These two are the same; but with different names; one is subtle and the other is splendour.

They are both mystique, flowing through the same wondrous and divine gate of universe.

Chapter 9

To fill up a cup to the brim, it will spill easily.

It is far better to stop pouring before it is full.

To sharpen a razor-sharp spear, the blade will get broken easily

To display a full household of precious treasures; it will never last long.

To boast your wealth and success will lead to your downfall with no one but yourself to blame.

To retire immediately after your achievement and success is wise; it is the way of nature.

Chapter 12

The five bright colours blind the eyes;

The five music notes deafen the ears;

The five fine foods dull the palate;

Too much entertainment will drive you delirious;

Too much desire and greed bring you misery.

Chapter 19

To abolish sagacity and discard sanctity; people will benefit a hundred fold.

To end false humanity and artificial benevolence, people will live in harmony and fidelity.

To stop scheming and gaining deceitful profit, theft and stealing will disappear.

It is not enough just to implement the above three rules.

Here I offer the true remedies to you;

Return to a simple and plain life and back to nature.

Be your true self and live a carefree and invulnerable life.

Chapter 33

To understand each other is clever and to know oneself is wise.

To conquer other's needs to be strong and to win over oneself has to be brilliant.

Content is wealth; perseverance leads to determination and nobility.

Do not go astray but cherish your true self and you will enjoy a long life.

Death is not the ending because your deed and your thought live forever.

Chapter 56

The wise will not preach; the one that will preach is unwise.

He is quiet and obscure; reserve his opinion and judgement to himself.

And brilliantly and subtly solves people's disputes.

This is what he will become, "The Tao", the Divine and Wondrous "Way" of the Universe.

No one should get too close to him;

No one should keep totally away from him;

Not to let him profit by you; not to be harmed by you;

No one can bring him glory; no one can bring him disgrace;

Such a person is the "World" and is honoured by all.

Summary

Chapter1
Both the nothingness of the Tao and everything of the world are the same. Both flow through the same Divine Gate of Wonderland.

Chapter9
Never do anything too extreme nor boast your wealth and success. To retire after your achievement is the only proper Way of Nature.

Chapter12
To the sage, moderation should apply to our Five Senses and that is the only and the best way to live a good life.

Chapter 19
To abolish all man made pretences, intelligence, laws and greed is not enough. You should return to Nature and live a simple and carefree life.

Chapter33
To live an eternal life, one must learn to understand oneself, be wise, brilliant, contented, and exist in harmony with Nature.

Chapter56
A truly wise man would be accepted and honoured by the world because he does not preach; he does not boast; he is simple and not greedy; always keeps a distance to either friend or foe.

The Summary of the above Summaries

Simple life is happy life. Return to Nature and live a life with moderation, sincerity and harmony; no pretences and no greed.

Brief Biography

It was said that Lao Tze was born in the year 571 B. C. His family name was Li and his first name was Er He was the native of Chu, a southern State during the Autumn and Spring Period. His life was rather obscure and legend said that Lao Tze's mother carried him for 12 months. (Some said 12 years)! When the day came, the baby had long white hair and wrinkled skin. That was why he was called Lao Tze which means old Master. His father was a veteran, wounded in battle and crippled for life. His mother was very able, weaving to support the family. Lao Tze was the only child of the family. His parents sent him to the best teacher to study. He was always an excellent student. Soon, he became a distinctive and learned man and acquired the great skill of astrology, genealogy, alchemy and herbal medicine. His fame travelled far and wide and was appointed to a public post by the state of Zhao He refused the proposal and left with his parents and his newly wedded wife. He spent the prime of his life as a gentleman-recluse. Until at the age of 57, the Emperor of Zhou invited him to his Court and appointed him as the royal court Librarian and historian. specializing in matters such as astrology and divination and in charge of the Royal Sacred Books. The Greatest Chinese Historian recorded in the Royal Chronicle, Shi-Chi, a Historical Meeting of the contemporary Younger Confucius and the Tough Old Master. It was a small, but formal State Visit of Confucius with his students and attendants. They travelled all the way from the State of Lu to the State of Zhou to ask Lao-Tze to tutor him in the knowledge of Ancient Rite, etc. Lao-Tze was not amused at the presence of the elaborate behaviour of Confucius and his company. He lectured Confucius for his pride and ambition. As for Confucius, we were told he was deeply impressed by this Old Sage. He did not show any sign of displeasure or disappointment. On the contrary, he praised Lao Tze and said,

Birds fly;
Fish swim;
Animals walk;
Dragon is obscure and divine;
Old Master is a Dragon with Wonder in and out and all around him.

At the age of 69, Lao Tze thought he had enough of this corrupted society and the evil of the royal court. Mounted on a green buffalo, he rode west and disappeared into the wilderness without saying good bye to anybody. Legend said that before he left civilization, on the request of a official, Van Hei at the Last Frontier Gate, Han Gu, he wrote a Booklet of 5000 words, putting down his philosophical teachings. After that, we never heard of anything about. him. No one knew where or when or how he died.

Brief Comment

The motto of this wandering philosopher Lao Tze is "Live a simple life; be free; be yourself and be close to nature." He is also a venerated scholar, but he is not a fighter. He denounces war, attacks taxation verbally and discards hypocrisy unreservedly. His talent and his reputation brought him to the prestigious position of the Chief Librarian of the Imperial Archives in the Capital of the Zhou Dynasty. He voluntarily went on exile twice in his working life!

Is he a pessimist or a defeatist? I am not sure. What I think for sure is that he is not a pusher nor an activist. His Tao Te Jing lectures people to take a "Let it be" attitude towards life. His Way 'Tao' is an invisible force, no violence but tolerance, no substance but eternity; no conqueror but a winner.

In the Han Dynasty, (202B. C. -220A. D.), the scholars of Orthodox Taoism thrived. Their doctrines of simplicity and return to nature developed into the state of quietude, sincerity and honesty in life. In fact, the Orthodox Taoism and Confucianism both bore the same torch to teach and both tried to reform the present society to a better future. Confucius was a reformer in education, a conformist in politics and a humanist in religious matters. In the case of Lao Tse, he kept himself to himself. He did not fight but meditate. He preached peace and tolerance. The Tibetan Monks and their principles are greatly influence by Orthodox Taoism. Eventually after 600 hundred years, Taoism was developed by a sect of religious fanatics who called themselves Taoists, the followers of Lao Tze. They adopted Tao Te Ching and called it their bible. Some of their followers sank to the level of superstitious practices. They claim Lao Tze as their religious founder and place him in the high altar and worshipped him, not just as a great philosopher, but as their god and supreme lord, a deity in the Taoists temple.

Carnelian gem imprint representing Socrates, Rome, 1st century
Socrates 470 BCE–399 BCE of Athens
Classical Greek philosopher.

Socrates was best known as a powerful influence upon the founders of Western philosophy, most particularly Plato and Aristotle, and while Socrates' principal contribution to philosophy is in the field of ethics, he also made important and lasting contributions to the fields of epistemology and logic. Socrates married a young woman, Xanthippe and had three sons, Lamprocles, Sophroniscus and Menexenus. When he was in prison, his friends arranged for him to escape. Socrates refused. He not only wished to avoid the pains of old age, but also to die because he "actually believed the right time had come for him to die." He accepted the poison and died in the prison cell at the age of 71, 399 BC. Like our Lao Tze, he was not a fighter but a winner contributing everlasting philosophy, beliefs and glory to mankind.

CHAPTER 5

Lun Yu (Analects)
(11 Verses) By Confucius and his Disciples

Confucius - The Greatest Teacher and The Arduous Minister

Foreword

According to Chinese tradition and to many people all over the world, Confucius is a great thinker, political philosopher, the founder of Confucianism and the greatest sage-teacher in China. After the death of Confucius, his disciples collected the fragments of his teachings and put into the text known to the Chinese, Lun Yu. It contains 29 Chapters and 452 verses and is mostly presented in short quotations or conversations between this great teacher and his student. Many of the verses are philosophical teaching. They are strikingly impressive. Most of these verses are short ethic-doctrines. A very clever and unique style for people easy to digest and quick to remember.

I think to talk (write) about Confucius even in general terms has to be divided into two perspectives. Firstly, he is idolized by all because most of his teaching was very good, short and nice, and was cleverly promoted by his able disciples. Secondly, throughout Chinese history, for more than two thousand years, he gained full support by the Imperial authority. Confucius was a very loyal subject. He promoted absolute obedience and loyalty to the Monarch, who had received the "Mandate of Heaven". He emphasised social harmony in the order of Heaven comes first, Earth second, the Throne third, the parents next and then the teacher. In return, after a few hundred years, all emperors promoted his Four Books and Five Classics as the curriculum of the Three Levels of Public Examination. They glorified him calling him, The Greatest Sage, "The Model Teacher and The Duke Laudably."

In fact, he made some mistakes during his political days. He paid for his mistakes dearly. At the age of 54, he was forced to resign. Wandering with his disciples from one state to another, he was very disappointed not being accepted to be an Imperial Court minister again! I hope my readers after reading this short foreword and this short translation will have a good picture about this Great Teacher. Looking at him, superficially and briefly, from two different angles, we can understand this sage as a great teacher and as an unsuccessful politician.

When I was a child, through the influence of my father, Confucius already entered my early life as the most learned man in Chinese cultural history, a great teacher, a very wise sage, a famous philosopher and a perfect man through and through. Day in and day out, I looked at those striking little posters pasted on the walls in our bed rooms, lounge and dinner area. We did not have a big house but big enough to house nearly half of the analects quotes. My father changed them by the season. They were never displayed in the bathroom nor in the kitchen. These places were disrespectful for the holy posters of our great sage. So under this most effective stereotype of learning, I adored and worshiped Confucius same as most of the people in China. But even when I was ten, I could never accept one quote which is about woman and petty people. (verse 29) My father defended him handsomely. He said, "Confucius was not a God! Sages do make mistakes because sages are human only."

Since. 2004, I have my own broadband at home. Life is much easier. I have never been that close to Confucius and to so many famous men in my life. It gave me confidence to include all the materials about our greatest sage whether it is positive or negative in my book. Confucius did make mistakes but he did pay for them. He provided a very good education to his students and in return, they spread his teachings all over the world now. Most effectively is the Analects. He made some mistakes in politics. He was not judged by the heads of the states opening but subtlety they all kept him at arms' length.

Confucius's contribution to us should be recognised in a fair and square level. Most of his simple and virtuous quotes do not just have an important moral impact to Chinese people, they also represent Chinese culture and Chinese value to many foreigners. I served two hours as a volunteer-in 'Age Concern'. I was so amazed to hear some little old ladies said to me, "Is that what Confucius says?"

Nowadays China is growing into a superpower, politically and economically. No wonder there are over 100 Confucius institutes around the world to provide opportunities for their students to learn the Chinese language and Chinese Culture; to read the great Chinese minds; and to study Confucius, the most influential philosopher and the greatest teacher of China.

In the 2008 Olympic Game, a high Communist Official suggested that in the Opening Ceremony, we should have a picture of Confucius to parade in front of the audience. I think it is a good suggestion! As a cultural figure to represent China, who can be more appropriate than this Great Teacher.

2008 Olympic Game

Original Text

Chapter 1

Verse 1 Confucius said:-

When I learn something, I practise it again and again. Surely it is a pleasure! Is it not so? When a friend comes to visit me from afar, is it not a very happy thing? Being ignored and not appreciated, I still feel unruffled and behaved calmly. This is what we call a perfect gentleman. Is it not?

Verse 4 Tsang Tze said:-

Everyday I examine myself repeatedly on three things. Firstly, have I not served people wholeheartedly? Secondly, have I been disloyal to my friends? Thirdly, have I diligently practised what I have learned from my teacher?

Chapter 2

Verse 4 Confucius said:-

When I was fifteen, I determined to learn and to study audaciously. When I was thirty, I have firmly and successfully established myself. When I was forty, I was unswayed by any illusions; everything is totally under control. When I was fifty, I acknowledged the Mandate of Heaven. When I was sixty, I humbly accepted all the good advices from people around me. When I am seventy, I will enjoy life following my heart's desire but within limits and moderation.

Chapter 7

Verse 19 Confucius said:-

The wise men enjoy the water. The benevolent people enjoy the mountain. The wise men are the active ones and the benevolent ones are the quiet men. The wise men are the jolly ones and the benevolent men live a long life.

Verse 16 Confucius said:-

Give me another 50 years to live, I will spend it studying the I Ching. Getting to know the I Ching better, I will be unlikely to make big mistakes and will keep me away from disasters.

Verse 21 Confucius said:-

When three friends walk together, there is always something to learn from each other. Follow the good ones; discard and correct the not so good ones.

Chapter 12

Verse 24 Tsang Tzu said:-

A gentleman makes friend through learning and appreciating literature together and in turn, helps everyone to promote virtue and benevolence.

Chapter 17

Verse 17 Confucius said

Never spread the 'hearsay' scandal. All virtuous gentlemen would despise and discard such scandalous behaviour.

Verse 29 Confucius said:-

It is most difficult to deal with women and small-minded man. If you get close to them, they become insolent and give you trouble. If you keep away from them, they start complaining.

Chapter 19

Verse 21 Tze Kung said:-

When a gentleman makes a mistake, it is like the eclipse of the Sun and the Moon and can be seen by everyone. When he corrects his mistakes, all men admire him. -

Verse 24 Confucius said:-

There is no way to become virtuous if you are gluttonously, eating day and night but doing nothing to exercise your mind and your body. There is plenty chess games and various kinds of sporting games around in the community. Is it not so? Would it be better for you to join in some of these games rather then idling and eating all day long?

Chinese Imperial Examination hall with
7500 cells, Guangdong, 1873.

Qilin (uicorn)

Qilin is a mythical hooved Chinese fanciful animal that is said to appear in conjunction with the arrival of a sage. It is a good omen that brings peace and prosperity. The earliest record of Qilin dates back to 5th BC, book Zuo Zhuan Legend has it that when Confucius was born, a unicorn appeared and brought him a piece of Jade. Before he died, a unicorn appeared again and escorted him to eternity.

Such is the absurb, superstituous and beautiful tale of the birth and death of Confucius It is one of the four Sacred Animals in China In ancient time, Dragon and Phoenix are Imperial Creatures of the Emperor and Empress. The Tortoise belongs to everybody, a peaceful but rather clumsy creature which brings good luck and longevity to people. Unicorn exists in Chinese mythology, 5000 years already. It is elegant and beautiful, a gentle beast with the body of a horse and a single, cute little horn in the middle of its forehead. It always brings people good omen.

Analects

After the death of Confucius, his disciples collected the fragments of his teachings and put into the text known to the Chinese, Lun Yu, Analects. It contains 29 Chapters and 452 verses and is mostly presented in short quotations or conversations between this great teacher and his student. Many of the verses are philosophical teaching. They are strikingly impressive. Most of these verses are short ethic-doctrines, a very clever and unique style for people easy to digest and quick to absorb.

Summary

In these verses Confucius and his students advise people how to be a benevolent gentleman and how to lead a jolly and virtuous life. In chapter 17 Verse 19, Confucius strongly condemns 'woman and petty-people.'

Brief Biography of Confucius

Confucius was born in the year 551 in County Qufu, the State of Lu. His personal name was Zhongni His first name was Qiu which means a hill and it was because he was born at the foot of a hill. His father, Shuliang, 10 feet tall, was a minor Army Officer whose first wife gave him nine daughters. His concubine gave him a son but was a cripple at birth. Eager for a healthy son, this old man at the age of 70, cohabitated with a young woman, Nganjing and successfully got themselves a son. His father died before Confucius was three. He was raised by his able mother and people believed that she was the descendent of Duke Zhou of Zhou Dynasty (1122-249 B. C.). Like his father, Confucius was 9 feet 6 inches tall. He went through a poverty- stricken childhood but never lack good education. Even as a child, he proudly played 'Leader' with other children and conducted a make -believe 'Temple Rituals Game' seriously with proper procedure. He was fond of music and sport, particularly in archery and fishing.

Once as a young scholar, he was refused entry to as society banquet for scholars given by a local noble-house just because of his ambiguous origin. Nevertheless, he redirected his energy to study. He worked very hard and learned thoroughly well the important Ancient Books, the Six Classics and the Six Arts. At the age of 16, he worked as an overseer in a granary and also taking care of animals in the farm and in the park. He married at the age of 19 and has one son and two daughters. He travelled a lot and started teaching at the age of 22. Soon, he earned a reputation of a good teacher, a gentleman of propriety and a knowledgeable scholar. His mother died in 527. B C. At the age of 35, as a junior adviser of Duke Zhao of Lu, he followed the Duke into exile and fled to the State of Qi. When he was 43, he returned to Lu and started teaching again. He also devoted his time to editing and compiling the Six Classics and the Six Arts etc. At 53, he was appointed by the new Duke Ting of Lu to be the Grand Secretary of Justice and later at the age of 56, promoted to be the Chief Minister of Lu. Despite of all the virtues his disciples praised him in the Analects, he was not a successful politician and was forced to resigned at the peak of his political power at the age of fifty-six. He spent the next thirteen years wandering from state to state; accompanying by a team of his faithful disciples. He always tried to re-establish feudalism, the good old order of ancient Zhou Dynasty. He tried very hard to persuade the other Rulers to accept his theory to reform, what he thought, the corrupted society. He tried to sell the old ethical value of etiquette, antiquity and his political philosophy but nobody wanted to listen to him. He was eager but over enthusiastic and thus got himself nowhere. At the end of thirteen long years, he realised his political life was over. He returned to Lu at the age of 67 (68) and continued to teach and to compile the classical-books. Confucius edited six ancient literary works, collectively known as the Six Classics. They are 1. The Odes 2. The Book of History 3. The Book of Rites 4. The Book of Music 5. I Ching 6. The Spring and Autumn Annals. He taught his student the 6 Classics as well as learning the skill of the 6 Arts which are 1. Rite. 2. Music 3. Archery 4. Horsemanship 5. Calligraphy 6. Mathematics.

He died at the age of 72; (73) and was buried in Qufu, his native County. At that time, he was not very well known in China. His reputation as a great philosopher and high esteem of teacher was totally promoted by his disciples after his death. If it wasn't for the disciples, his name would never be so very well known to the rest of the World.

Brief Comment

Confucius was a Great Teacher and a Famous Philosopher for more than two thousand years in China. Now in the 21st Century, his doctrines and his moral values, in the name of Confucianism, was well spreading all over the world. As a teacher, he was successful. He was the first teacher in China to open public schools, and accept any student, who came to him. Before him, there was only private schools or private tutors for the children of the Nobles and Rich people. It is said that out of his 3000 students, he selected 72 as his close disciples. Confucius taught them to follow his ethical codes to become gentlemen and they had to learn the Six Classics and the Six Arts. Many of these 72 students became Confucius's loyal disciples.

During the long 13 years of his exile from State to State, these disciples went through imprisonment and starvation with him but still stood close to him faithfully. When Confucius died, his disciples worked very hard and succeeded to promote him from a small philosopher and good teacher to a sage

When Confucius was 56, he was in politics for a few years. He was too eager to reform the ancient etiquette and too straight and severe for his opponents. Even it was a total failure, his students shared his moment of glory as well as his moment of dispair with him. When he started his long exile, they accompanied him with the hope of being employed by a new Duke again. After thirteen years, in despair and disappointment, they went home. These brilliant young men; some were ambitious administrators; some were political genius; some were clever in legal matter; some were financial experts; some were eloquent speakers; many were masters in literature. With a great team like this, they worked together and managed to compile a superb Analects; it is short; it is striking; it is easy to remember. The dialogues and the quotations between the teacher and the students are interesting and handsome; humane and simple to absorb.

Confucius and the Great Greek Philosophers, Socrates, Aristotle and Plato, were all great teachers and they were world class philosophers. They all lived a few hundred years before Christ but The Analects was so simple, and so very easy to interpret that there is no comparison to the deep and academic structure of Plato's Symposium and Phaetons.

The Analects easily become the scholars' great book as well as a household moral Guide because more than two third of the contents are plain and short mottos. Even laymen can easily digest it. I remember when I was a little girl, my home was full of Confucius' short mottos. My father wrote these small posters and pasted them on the walls. Every now and then he recited them out loud and explained to us. As a five year old child, I muttered, "How Boring!"

Taoism is too abstract! Buddhism is too negative and it is foreign. After hundred years, the imperial court of the Han Dynasty (202 BC-202 AD) looking for a State Cult, naturally turned to the popular local teacher. He was always loyal to the Imperial Throne and he was no longer living! Dead men do not bite! Quite conveniently, they turned him into a sage and a god! They built him impressive temples and shrines; they bestowed on him some grand titles; they invented the absurd and fantastical two meetings of the sacred unicorn, one bringing him a piece of jade, signifying the birth of Confucius was blessed with the Mandate of Heaven and the second meeting was before his death. Confucius's disciples had done another superb thing, not only successfully promoted him as a sage and a small god beyond imagination but also created an everlasting enterprise, giving his home town, Qufu one of the best and most profitable tourist attractions in China.

Personally I respect him as a great teacher and admired him having such a wonderful and able team of disciples to promote him. As I learnt from many books and many web pages I realise even a benevolent sage and a humane teacher, could be a different person, when involved in politics. He tried very hard to be a good politician but he failed. He was in power for a short time only. He did not have the subtlety and the capacity to be a statesman. The complex court life was different from preaching the obedient students and editing the tedious classics in the quiet corner of a comfortable class room. He was thirsty for power but had not got the skill to govern and to survive in the political arena. After wandering for thirteen years, he ended his self-exile odyssey as a rather unhappy teacher in his home town. Ironically, when he was gone, the political propaganda machine in Han Dynasty used his name and gave him the full glory and fame which he had pursuit many years during his life time but in vain. From then on, all the Imperial Courts put The Six Classics and later 13 Classics, as the main curriculum for the Imperial 3 levels Examinations; the County, the Provincial and the Palace. I think the people of the Warring States Period were lucky to have him as a great teacher.

Aristotle (384 BC – March 7, 322 BC) was a Greek philosopher, a student of Plato and teacher of Alexander the Great. Along with Socrates and Plato, Aristotle was one of the most influential of ancient Greek philosophers. Some consider Plato and Aristotle to have founded two of the most important schools of Ancient philosophy. After spending several years tutoring the young Alexander, Aristotle returned to Athens. And established his own school. Same as our sage,Confucius, they were great teachers and influential philosophers. They both died of natural cause in their homeland at a good old age.

CHAPTER 6

Mencius
A Dialogue Between Mencius and King Wai of
Liang By Mencius

A Devoted Disciple of Confucius (372-289 B. C.)
Mencius visited the Warring States
following the route of Confucius

Foreword

Mencius was generally regarded as the greatest Confucian thinker after Confucius himself. He was also named the Second Sage after Confucius. He was not just a political philosopher and a teacher but followed the footstep of Confucius as a wandering elite. A very ambitious and reverend scholar, Mencius dedicated all his life in glorifying Confucius and declared as long as he lived he would follow, defend and spread the teaching of his supreme master, Confucius. He visited many minor states during the Warring States Period. He preached to the rulers the traditional virtues of the ancient dynasties but never received a sympathetic hearing. His lofty doctrine was too impractical for the power struggled warlords. After 40 years, same as Confucius, he returned home in despair to write and to teach.

Mencius was best known for the view that "human nature is good." Nevertheless, this view was challenged by Xunzi (third century BC), another major Confucian thinker, who defended the alternative view that "human nature is evil". Until modern times, these two influential and intellectual Confucian thoughts are subject to argument.

'Mencius' was included as one of the Four Books, which became canonical texts of the Confucian tradition. Since then, Mencius teachings have been very influential on the development of Confucian thought up to modern times. "Mencius" is a Confucian classic recording the words of Mencius. This chapter is his well known first political meeting in his advisory capacity. Obviously, he thought he had done well and recorded it in the first chapter of Mencius. In fact to look at it at a different angle, could this be the root of his 40 years unsuccessful political career.

The Meeting of Mencius and King Wei of Liang
The Humble King

The Humble King of Liang received His Guest, Mencius,
with respect. He sought advice from the renowned scholar.

This is the first chapter of 'Mencius':

On one occasion, Mencius went to see King Wei of Liang. As soon as he arrived, the King received him warmly at his Court and began the conversation. The King said, "Sir, you have travelled thousand of miles to come here. I presume you must have something to profit my Kingdom."

Mencius replied, "Why must your majesty talk about profit! What I come to offer you are some advics about benevolence and righteousness.

If the King talks of nothing but how to profit his Kingdom, soon his ministers will also talk about how to profit his family. The lower officials and the common people will follow suit, scrambling around looking and asking for profit for themselves. The Kingdom will be in danger and eventually it might fall.

In the Kingdom of ten thousand chariots, the prince who kills the king would come from the thousand chariots. The rebel of a thousand chariot would be killed by the hundred chariot-chief. All these from ten thousands to thousand, from a thousand to hundred are in a good proportion of struggling for power.

If one puts profit in front of virtue, he will never be satisfied unless he snatches all of it. He is not a real benevolent man if he does not care for his parents. There is also no virtuous man if he puts his King in second place. Therefore it is better for your Majesty to devote all your time to talk about virtue and benevolence, the only themes in our speech. I do not see why we should bring the word 'profit' into our conversation.

Summary

Mencius went to see King Wei of Liang. The King received him warmly at his Court and asked how to obtain profit for his Kingdom.

Mencius refused to talk about profit. He insisted that Virtue and Benevolence were the only themes of his conversation.

Brief Biography

Mencius was born in the State of Zou, 371 B. C., approximately one hundred years after the death of Confucius. His father died when he was about three years old. He was raised by his able mother, Mother Meng who has since become an inspiration and a model-mother to countless Chinese mothers. The most famous story about this remarkable woman was how she moved her home three times to ensure her son would grow up in what she considered a proper environment. He received his education from Tzu Szu, grandson of Confucius. As a self-appointed protector of Confucius' original ideas, he devoted his life to spread the Doctrine of Confucianism and made sure it would become the most important and influential philosophy in the history of China. In personality, he was completely different from Confucius. Confucius was a man of few words and disliked public speaking. Mencius was eloquent and enjoyed giving lectures to a large audience. Whereas Confucius was straight forward, Mencius would argue sharply and wittingly. Confucius had managed not too much material gains, but Mencius enjoyed living his life in comparative luxury. In teaching, Confucius liked to use the examples of people to demonstrate to his students. Mencius liked to use animals and anecdotes. Both of them worshiped the Sage Kings, Yao, Shun, Yue. They praised them admiringly to their students. Confucius taught love and virtue to his students and emphasised how to cultivate them while Mencius taught his students that men are born good, and it is up to the environment to develop these inborn goodness of mankind. In politics, the two Sages are traditionalists and both are court- advisers. Both travelled from court to court. But Mencius was far more successful than Confucius in material gain. He was travelled by 80 smart chariots and while his predecessor Confucius only went round in a dozen chariots. Nevertheless all these display of vanity got him to nowhere in politics. At the age of 65, he realised the same as Confucius, that his position was with his disciples and his books at his hometown. The ruling class would only treat him with courtesy and paid him well. Same as all the rest of thousands of the wandering advisers, the Royal Courts never gave them political power but gave them a very high pay. In those days keeping advisers was fashionable in the Royal Courts. The more famous scholars and countless talented people kept in Court, the more louder, would the Kings boast to their neighbouring rivals.

The Warring States Period was a chaotic time of power struggle and also an affluent-time of material and cultural development. The Kings were too busy in fighting the constant territorial-battles and involving themselves to the enjoyment of material luxury than to listen to the lofty and boring lectures on antiquity and humane government of this old Sage. Again same as Confucius, he returned home at, gaining fame and riches but no political power. He spent the rest of his life writing and teaching. He died at a good old age of 84.

A famous Chinese idiom Mencius' mother moves three times:
A traditional legend that Mencius' mother moved their house three times from beside a cemetery to beside a marketplace, to finally beside a school. This idiom refers to the importance of a proper environment for the proper upbringing of children.

Brief Comment

Mencius dedicated all his life in glorifying Confucius and declared as long as he lived he would follow and spread the teaching of his supreme master, Confucius. Same as Confucius, he preached to the Kings the traditional virtues of the ancient dynasties but never received a sympathetic hearing. Their lofty doctrine was too impractical for the power struggle of the War-lords. Again, in despair, he returned home to teach and to write. He successfully compiled the anthology which bears his name and relates the vivid conversations and arguments of Kings and Princes. We can see that Mencius was a shrewd self-promoter. He followed up the popular Concept of Confucius' benevolence and virtue Doctrines and won good favour in the intellectual world of the Confucians. His book 'Men Tze' conveyed striking pictures of the meeting of the king and the sage! I wondered would the King be amused if he read it! Personally, I think the King was a good King and he asked good questions! He cared for his kingdom and his people. "Profit" is not stealing and is not cheating! "Profit" is not robbing and is not done by force. According to Mencius, he said, 'It is the duty of a King to look after his people and provide them a good living; the old should be clothed in silk and have meat on their dinner table.' Obviously, in so doing, the King requires a wealthy and healthy 'Bank' in the Kingdom. The only way to ensure and secure it is to 'make profit' and so it would enable him to improve the prosperity of the Kingdom! I was taught of this essay when I was about twelve. Even as a young student, I could not fully agree to this argument. Mencius was a reasonably rich and happy man. He died at the age of 84, and indeed accomplished his dream to glorify Confucianism successfully. He has been known in China as "The Second Sage".

The Great Disciple of Jesus-Paul of Tarsus (b. c. 10, d. c. 67)-

According to Acts, Paul was born in modern-day Turkey, Unlike the Twelve Apostles, Paul never met Jesus before the crucifixion. Same as Mencius who had never met Confucius but claimed to be Confucius' greatest disciple. Paul's conversion took place as he was traveling the road to Damascus, and experienced a vision of the resurrected Jesus. Mencius followed Confucius' route visiting states far and wide in style during the Warring period to spread his doctrines. He failed his mission and was rejected politely by all the kings.

The 14 Epistles in the New Testament are traditionally attributed to Paul. Paul of Tarsus (b. *c.* 10, d. *c.* 67), the *Apostle to the Gentiles,* was, together with Simon Peter, the most notable of Early Christian missionaries. Paul was thrown into prison twice. Eventually, as a martyre, he was beheaded in the year 67.

CHAPTER 7

The Butterfly Dream
Written by Zhuang Zhou 369-286 b. c.

The famous Chinese Dreamer Zhuang Zhou

Foreword

Zhuang Tze is the only dynamic and eccentric sage in classical Chinese literary world. This Great Taoist philosopher is unique. Nowhere in early Chinese literature do we have such a wealth of satire, allegory and poetic fantasy. It is all attributed by this remarkable genius. He is a naturalist, a dreamer, a strong believer in fate and natural phenomena. He believes in no God but believes in Tao, (The Way and The One) which is everything, everywhere and timeless.

In his extreme philosophy, he advises people to lead a simple, decent and carefree life. He emphases that life should be enjoyed and death should not be feared. To him everything in life is subject to the eternal transformation. A simple life is a happy life. He playfully put forth his mystical and fatalistic ethic in his entire beautiful and humorous extravaganza. Thus he not just followed Lao Tze but trod on his path to the extreme, adding fantasies-charms and vibrant imaginations to the dull and severe doctrines of his contemporaries. Nearly all the scholars, the failures, in the society turn to Zhou for consolation. As scapegoats, these fatalistic elements and escapism theory provides them plenty of channels to face the world comfortably if not with pride and satisfaction. He harboured these poor souls and gave them peace and harmony in their adversity. His butterfly dream is the most beautiful and also is the only fantastic and fairy-like dream in Chinese classical literature. Thanks to him, every now and then this essay generates myriad soft warm beams shining romantically with a happy butterfly dancing under the silvery moon.

Chapter 7 The Butterfly Dream

It was at the twilight of the evening. Zhuang Zhou dozed off and dreamt that he had turned into a flitting happy butterfly.

Fluttering and flitting here and there, he enjoyed to be a carefree butterfly very much indeed. He had completely forgotten that he was Zhou.

All of a sudden he woke up and he was Zhou again. Then he was puzzled and confused. He did not know for sure if he was Zhou dreaming to become a Butterfly or he was the butterfly dreaming to become Zhou.

Between Zhou and the butterfly, there must be a dividing line somewhere!

This Transition is what is called, "The Transformation of Material Things."

Summary:

Zhou dreamt that he was a happy butterfly. When he woke up, he wondered whether he was a butterfly or a butterfly dreaming to be him. He called it the transformation of things.

Brief Biography

Zhou was the personal name of Zhuang Tze. This eccentric Sage, one of the Greatest Taoist philosopher and writer was born around the year 369 BC. approximately in the State of Song, County Meng. There was very little record about his life. All we know about him is that he was married and had children. He was a minor official in his home county, Meng, but not for long. He was always poor and had been a hawker selling corns and sandals. He was so very poor that when he was invited to see King Ngai, he wore patched shoddy clothes and shabby holly shoes. The King felt sorry for him looking so miserable. Nevertheless, he proudly declared to the Court that he might be poor but he was definitely not miserable. He lived in a little humble hut at the back of a little humble lane. One day he had to borrow some rice to feed the family. Another day King Wei of Chu sent him gold and invited him to be his minister. He refused both offer with a smile.

When his wife died of good old age, he sang and beat on a basin to show his carefree attitude and platonic feeling towards life. He also told his disciples that when he died he did not want a Traditional Proper Burial. He would like to have a 'Natural Funeral'; that is to place his naked body in the open to feed the birds and animals. He was one of the greatest Taoist philosopher and was best known through his Book, 'Zhuang Tze.' It composed of 35 chapters and people belief that the first 7 chapters are genuinely written by this great Sage. Although he was skin and bone and lived in poverty, he died a happy old man of 82.

Brief Comment

According to Zhou, everything was in process of destruction and everything was in process of construction. There was no present or past; forget about the conventional laws and rules and follow your good instinct to be in the path of Tao-Way. He was always poor but he was never a bitter man. He lived happily in his fantasy land and led others to share and to enjoy his Great mystic and humour in his witty essays. He wrote the 'Chaung Tze' (zhuang) and had some loyal disciples followed to help to create his Dreams.

'Zhaung Tze' is a Taoist Text with a difference. In 'Tao Te King', Lao Tze had no time for light hearted illustrations but 'Zhuang Tze' was funny most of the time. In his allegory and satire, its animals, insects, birds, fishes, plants etc were larger than life. What a vivid imagination!

The first 7 chapters of his book "Zhuang" were written by the master himself and the other 43 were written by his faithful disciples. On the literary point of view, we admire his essays very much indeed! It was said that his poetic essays were like diamonds sparkling in the dim literary-sky. We yearn for Zhou's dreamy rhythm and his mystical charms. He had not just captured the imagination of many Chinese for thousands of years; even 'The Father of Modern Chinese Writers,' Lu Xun(迅) adored him and the great English writer Oscar Wilde praised him. As for us, little people, we admired him. The motto of Zhou is, 'Blessed are the Free and Simple; Genuine and Gleeful. They shall see the Kingdom of Tao' (Zhou's butterfly land).

Zhou Shuren, a very famous writer and an admirer of Zhuang Tze,

Zhou was an admirer of Zhuang Tze. Lu Xun was his pen name (September 25, 1881 – October 19, 1936) Lu Xun was one of the most influential Chinese writers of the 20th century. He was hailed as 'The father of the Chinese Modern Writer and was considered to be the founder of modern Chinese literature. Lu Xun was a teacher, a very successful short story writer, editor, translator, critic, renowned Essayist and one of the extreme Left-Wing writers. He was among the early supporters of the Esperanto movement in China.

Lu Xun died in 1936 of tuberculosis in Shanghai. He was survived by a son, Haiying. Before he died, he told his young son never to be a writer. The reason fo saying this was rather complicated. We speculated that he enjoyed writing but hecause of his out-spoken, and his Left Wing political attitude, he made enemies. He had to seek shelter and refugeed in Shanghai All these worries, pressure and stress were some of the causes that shortened his life.

His style of wrting is very powerful; always sharp, ironic and incisive; but sincere and straightword. He roused the righteous social conscious of the young people of the litrerary world and led them to communism. Lu Xun worked hard and lived a relatively short life. He died at the age of 55. Zhaung Tze died at the age of 82. Does it seem strange for a conscientious fighter like Lu Xun to admire our eccentric, carefree and happy butterfly man?

During my teens, reading was my only hobby and I spent all my pocket money in buying books. I had a whole collection of Lu Xun and Chairman Mo's work. Partly under their influence, I was an angry youth, not bitter but very aggressive and quarrellsome. Luckily, nothing went too extreme. I abandoned all these collections at my late teens. My 'Happy Dreamland' led me to a land of moonlight and honey. I think I turn to the Butterfly man for the rest of my life. I stick to his short and sweet motto, "Life is short! Life is beautiful."

The Dream King from Israel:

Joseph gained power and riches by interpreting dreams for the Pharaoh.

Joseph is a well known figure in the Book of Genesis in the Old Testament. He was Jacob's eleventh son. He is famous for his God-given ability to interpret dreams. Out of sheer jealousy, his brothers sold young Joseph to Egypt into slavery for twelve pieces of silver. Eventually he gained power and riches by interpreting dreams for the Pharaoh and became his chief adviser. During a big famine, his brothers came to Egypt to buy gain from Joseph. Joseph forgave his brothers and promised that he would provide for their wants. He lived to the age of one hundred and ten, and saw his great-grandchildren grow up. Our butterfly man died a happy man at the age of 82.

CHAPTER 8

The Art of War
By Sun Tzu Approx. 5th century BC

Sun Tzu —a Great Scholar General of China

Foreword

Sun Tzu (ca 6th century BC) was the author of The Art of War. He was a great historical general and also a famous scholar of the military arts. The Spring and Autumn peroid of China (722–481 BC) was a time of constant warfare between seven nations (Qin, Chu, Wu, Chi, Han, Wei and Yan) seeking to control all of China. Sun Tzu was a heroic general and his victories inspired him to write the Art of War. It wa an instant success and widely accepted as a masterpiece on strategy and has been referenced by generals and theorists throughout history. The book was not only popular among military theorists, but also among political leaders and. business managers. Theories of battle are essential in times of war, but the text also helps to council diplomacy and cultivate relationships with other nations in time of peace. Sun Tzu's The *Art of War* has been deeply influential. throughout Chinese history as well as global super-powers. Japan was the first country to borrow Sun Tzu's military tactics in the Nara Era (693-755). France was the first country translated this book thoroughly into French in the year 1769. It was said that Emperor Napoleon used many of its strategies to win his battles in Europe. In 1910 the English version was published. Later, there are also German, Russian, Korean and Hebrew translations. We were told that during the 1991 Gulf War in the middle east, General H. Norman Schwarzkopf, the Commander of the U. S and Allied Forces, in the battle of Desert Storm, used 'The Art of War' to direct his soldiers and officers. The general put to practice Sun Tzu's principles of deception, speed, and attacking the enemy's weakness. It turned out to be a brilliant Victory of the Allied Forces in Modern War History.

I know some rather unhappy people. They are not young. They work hard and when they retire they are reasonably rich but physically they are not well at all. They look morbid. They always complain aches and pains here and there and everywhere. They keep a copy of The Art of War as their bedtime reading book and apply the War Theories as golden rules to their livelihood. Personally, I will never get too close to these big war game theories. This book is written for warlords, generals, strategists, political leaders and chairmen of corporations. We little people should keep to our simple and honest way of life; stick to our artless and open attitude to people around you. Never consider yourself charging in the Battle of Waterloo. You will never be truly happy if you think you are living in Desert Storm or in Waterloo.

Please always remember Deception and Scheming poisons ones mind and body. There is a most famous quotation (chapter 1, paragraph 18) of Sun Tzu:

All warfare is based on deception.

Excerpt from Chapter 8:

Sun Tzu said, 'In the Art of War, when the general receives the order from his king to go to battle, he would have to bring together his soldiers and organise his army ready to fight.

1. He must not station the camp on lowland.

2. He must make friends with the intersecting-highways of the neighbouring States.

3. He must not stay in a solitary country.

4. He must rely on warfare-strategy when he falls to a hemmed-in situation.

5. He must fight his way out when he is in a treacherous place.

6. There are routes where one must not follow.

7. There are forces which one must not attack.

8. There are cities where must not surrender.

9. There are places which one must not challenge.

At times, there are orders even from the King which one must not obey. The General who understands these 9 Tactics of War, knows The Art of War.

According to the Historical Record, King Wu sent Sun 180 of his Palace Ladies to be trained into fighting soldiers. At first these ladies laughed and giggled messing around boisterously. After the execution of two of the King's favourite ladies, the Captains, the King and the rest of the ladies were horrified; but shortly after, General Sun accomplished his mission. The lady-troop was trained successfully in good order. Sun had proved he was not just a famous brilliant Military Writer but also a Great Amy Genius in practical training and drilling as well as in Writing.

With great anger and sadness, the King was horrified but still tolerated this anguish event and appointed Sun as his general-in-command. Afterwards, Sun won many battles for King Wu. When the King died, his grandson (son?) came to the throne. Sun still kept on fighting for the new King.

Summary

On Chapter 8 of 'The Art of War', Sun Tzu explained 9 tactics to his soldiers and instructed them where, when and how to fight a sure-win battle including not to obey the King's order at time in the war zone.

Brief Biography

Sun Tzu was the courtesy name of Sun Wu. Wu was his first name. His personal name was Chang Qing. Although he was the greatest military strategist in China, we know very little about his personal life. Even his date of birth and his date of death were not identified. He came from the State of Chai of a well-known military noble family. His ancestors' family name was Tin. In the year 672 BC. Sun's grandfather won the Battle of Loi for the Duke of Chai against the State of Chu. He was awarded by the Duke the Territory of Lok On and also granted him a new surname Sun. Later, the State of Chai was torn in Civil war and Sun had to flee to The State of Wu, living as a semi-hermit Farmer. In the year 521 BC, he was strongly recommended by his best friend, Minister Wu Tzu Hsu to serve the King of Wu. Sun accepted the invitation. Eventually he proved himself that he was a superb military strategist as well as a great military general. He won many battles for the King. 10 years later, the King died of injuries in fighting. Sun remained in court to serve the new King Fu Chai, who was the grandson of King Wu. Sun carried on to fight for Fu. In the year 484BC, he won a victorious battle against the State of Chi. Finally, in the year 482 BC. The State of Wu became one of the five dominant powers during the Spring and Autumn Period. The late

King's dream was at last accomplished by Sun. Sun Tzu is not only a superb Military General in ancient China but also the reputed writer of 'The Art of War', the world-wide military masterpiece. "The Art of War" was written by Sun Tzu during the Spring and Autumn Period (770-476BC). He was praised as the founder of military science, and the book also has been recognised as the best military writings in China. The book consisted of 13 chapters, containing all the basic principles and superb military tactics; including military psychology and military planning. It is considered to be the greatest military treasure in China.

Comment

The tactics and the strategies in his book played a very important part in reshaping Chinese History. Japan was the first country to borrow Sun Tzu's military tactics in the Nara Era (693-755). France was the first country translated this book thoroughly into French in the year 1769. It was said that Emperor Napoleon used many of its strategies to win his battles in Europe. In 1910 the English version was published. Later, there are also German, Russian, Korean and Hebrew translations. We were told that during the 1991 Gulf War in the middle east, General H. Norman Schwarzkopf, the Commander of the U. S. and Allied Forces, using 'The Art of War' to teach his soldiers and officers. It was a brilliant victory of the Allied Forces in modern war history. During the European Football Championship in 2004, the Portuguese coach, (now the Chelsea FC coach) Luiz Felipe Scolari always carried Sun's book in his pocket and often quoted from it during team training. The Art of War' is artistic, philosophical, scientific and operational. It is truly our national pride. Sun Tzu was a man of mystery. Nobody knows when he died, how he died, where he died and why he died.

We hope the execution of the two King's Lady-Captains was not true. After all there was no big offence, no corruption, no treachery and no manslaughter involved. The penalty for giggling, laughing and messing around is Death which is far too severe! It is cruel! It is unjust! It is most unwise! It is barbaric! You could strip off these ladies. titles. You could give them a heavy fogging. You could imprison them for a few months or even a few years. We agree that War is cruel! War is ugly!

War is horrible! War is deceptive! But these ladies were only the King's toy soldiers! They were not at war! We Chinese always boast ourselves a Great Civilized Country and Sun Tzu was suppose to be a rational General. This is not civilized by any standard. Most probably, people invented a sensational story to impress the ignorant and the boring multitude. This is definitely one of the tasteless, senseless and most inhumane dramas in history.

The Art of War
In a bamboo book around early Han Dynasty

In 1972 a set of bamboo engraved texts were discovered in a grave near Linyi in Shandong. The Art of War may have been written between 400 BC and 320 BC. It is an immensely influential ancient Chinese book on military strategy. It is said that Cao Cao, Napoleon, Joseph Stalin, Mao Zedong and General H. Norman had all read and influenced by this great book.

The first recorded battle in the history of China:

The first important recorded warfare in the history of China is where Yellow Emperor defeated Chiyou, and settled with his tribe Huaxia in 2600BC.

The military history of China extends from around 1500 BC to the present day. China has the longest continuous development of mulitary history in the world. Like the Chinese History it is divided into three periods: 1. ancient China (c. 1500-221 BC), 2. Imperial China (221 BC-1912), and 3. Modern China (1912-present)

Hannibal -The African General from Carthage

Hannibal, (247 BC – ca. 183 BC) is universally regarded as one of the greatest military commanders and tacticians in history. His most famous achievement was at the invasion of Italy in the year 206 BC. He marched an army, which included war elephants, acrossing the Alps and into northernItaly. Hannibal successfully crossed the mountains, despite numerous obstacles but at a very heavy cost. He won and marched into northern Italy but with only half the forces he had started with; out of his 76 war elephants, only a few elephants left. Later in his defeated in a naval battle, he fled. In the year 183BC, rather than surrendered to the Roman he committed suicide. I wonder could Sun Tzu help him to be a more successful general and died a happier death.

CHAPTER 9

Monkey King
Introduction of The Four Great Chinese Classics
- Novels: 1. Monkey King 2. Red Chamber
Dream 3. Three Kingdoms 4. Water Margin

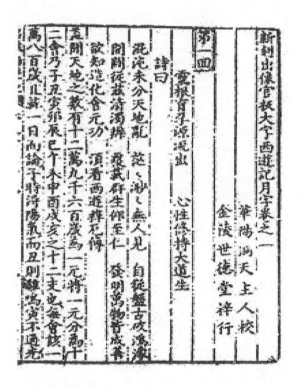

A block print of Journey to the West 16th century.

Preface

Nearly all Chinese are influenced by the tales of their Four Great Classic Novels. They are **1.** The Journey to the West **2.** The Dream of the Red Chamber **3.** Romance of the Three Kingdoms **4.** Water Margin Even illiterate Chinese are familiar with the plots, the characters and all the heroes and heroines. They learn from different sources such as story tellers, movies, theatres and television. These novels are long and all have over hundred chapters with the exception of Water Margin which has only 71 chapters.

Out of these four novels, The Journey to the West is probably the most popular and influential in China and in South East Asia. It is highly imaginative and mythological and tells the journey of a monk, accompany by three animals disciples, to bring the Buddhist sutras from India back to China.

The Red Chamber has 120 chapters. It depicts a sad love story among three teenage cousins in the opulent household of a noble family. The novel has a very large number of characters, more than 400 people in a magnificent setting, the Grand View Park. It is considered to be the best novel ever written in Chinese Literature. Cao Xueqin (1715?-1763), the author died sometime in 1763, leaving his novel in a very advanced stage of completion. He was survived by a wife and at least a son.

The Romance of the Three Kingdoms is a historical novel, combining fiction with real life events, with brilliant military strategies, countless battles and fierce warriors. Some people believe that it is a great historical narrative not just a novel. Water Margin tells the story of 108 outlaws. This bandit group kills, fights, robs and steals from the rich and corrupted officials. They are supposed to help the weak and the poor. But some of them are brutal and evil. The glorification of the underworld caused the book to be banned by the Authority during the Ming Dynasty.

Throughout my childhood, reading novels was my favourite past time. These four great novels stimulated me with their profound imagination and provided me with a deep understanding of the ancient Chinese way of life and tradition. My young mind was filled with these heroes and villains, monsters, deities and the mighty gods and goddesses. Living within these magnificent books, there was never a dull moment. Even in my dreams, I dreamt vividly of my complex story-land. They were colourful and happy dreams; I fought the evil on the side of the good and always won because in the end God always intervened. I like to think that I am above average in confidence, exceptionally optimistic, always cheerful, rather humble and a hopeless dreamer. Even now I am over 70 years old, subconsciously I am still partly influenced and affected by the novels I read. Whether on open display or hinding indirectly, deep in my heart I believe that God is everywhere. Good for goodness sake or good for God's sake become my motto. My fantasy land is healthy and imaginative.

Here, I present a brief introduction, my commentary and summary of a few excerpts of these 4 great novels. My main aim is to offer you a bird's-eye view of these long novels in a very short form. To read the original is time consuming. My introduction is brief enough for you to appreciate and to enjoy the beauty of these great books within just an hour or less. Later, if you have the time and the interest, please go to the libraries or book shops to get the original. I will put down some of the names of the translators of these novels at the end of this text.

To me, there is so much similarity between The East and West in some classical novels and literature. When I started reading The Hobbit, I could not stop myself thinking of all the imaginary scenery and monsters along the route of Tang Monk and compared to the hazardous journey of the Hobbits of the West to the journey of the Monkey King of the East.

We all know about Robin Hood the Lord of Sherwood Forest. Our 108 'Chinese Robin Hood' in Water Margin are doing more or less the same job, to help the poor and to fight against corrupt authority but our outlaws are not merry men. Most of them are bitter and brutal.

War and Peace is a great War Epic in the West and the Romance of the Three Kingdoms is the greatest and the longest military and historical novel ever written in the East. As for Red Chamber, it is great and has no match in length of any love story in Chinese literature. Shakespeare's Tragedies are short and striking and more well known in the global literary circle.

Foreword

The Journey to the West (The Story of the Monkey King), is written by Wu Cheng Eng, 1504-1582. It is the Chinese people's favourite story book and in it, the most extraordinary Monkey King is everybody's Celestial Hero. It is based on the partly true story of a famous Monk, Triptaka. With the blessing of the 7th Century Tang Emperor and the helping of three animal-disciples and a divine horse, Triptaka took 12 long years to travel to India to bring back to China the original copy of the Buddhist Scriptures. This long novel has 100 chapters and is a combination of facts and myth; religion and fantasy; loyalty and faith; wit and absurdity; humour and romance; treachery and betrayal; monsters and numerous deities including Buddha and the Goddess of Mercy.

Monkey King, Sun Wu Kung, is Tang Monk's most able disciple. He is rebellious and very restless; extremely intelligent and agile, possesses supernatural power; full of wit and humour; utterly faithful to his Master. He is the pillar of strength of this pilgrimage. Pigsy, ranks next to Monkey King. This grotesque looking creature is lazy and weak in faith; has great physical strength; is a womaniser with a kind heart and a big appetites. He is humorous and brings smile and laughter to all. Very often he betrays his fellow disciples and is unfaithful to his Master. So the Monkey King always has to keep an eye on him. Sandy, is the quiet one. He is sincere and obedient; meek and humble. He is not the mighty fighter like Monkey King and he can hardly protect his Master from the demons and evil spirits but he is a loyal and good companion to the Master and always willingly to perform all the manual work.

The pilgrims encounter countless demons, ogres, monsters and ghosts. The team has to fight for their lives all the time; they suffer; they struggle, they flee and hide; very often they have to turn to Heaven for help. They also have to cross numerous treacherous rivers and dangerous mountains; countless traps and snares set by the evil demons and ogres; hazardous frozen-grounds; burning deserts and destructive volcanoes. Altogether they have to face 81 challenges and one by one, through their loyalty, determination, bravery, devotion, perseverance, magical powers, superhuman abilities and with the assistance of Buddha and the gods, the team triumphantly defeats all the adversities. These 81 marvellous adventures sometimes convey a little bit of moral lessons of Confucius and Taoist philosophy to enlightening their body and soul. But Buddha always has the last say and is their one and only one Salvation. These three elements of Chinese religious synthesis, Confucianism, Taoism and Buddhism are the main theme and framework of this great novel

Out of the four great novels, this religious fantasy and imaginative masterpiece is probably the most popular and entertaining classic novel and is best loved by the people in China. We like and adore The Heavenly Monkey King. With the religious basis of a saintly monk, it branches out into many beautiful fairly-tales as well as mythological satire, full of humour, wit and philosophical wisdom mixing Chinese tradition and culture. It is a delightful and wholesome novel that has hardly any obscenity nor brutality. We Chinese are quite familiar with all the characters in the novel. We grow up with many of these household names; The Supreme Goddess of Mercy, the Paramount Uppermost Buddha, the bad and evil, the good and divine spirits; the strong and weak, the gentle and solemn deities.

Above all, the Immortal Monkey King captures the hearts of many families. We are fascinated by his romantic background; we admire his might and magic; we respect his kindness towards the weak especially his subjects-the little monkeys; we enjoy his good humour and tricks. Subconsciously, we worship this Monkey King even though he is only a fictional creature in a novel. I was so happy when my mother told me that Monkey King is my god father. She was a midwife and supposed to be very scientific. But when I was very ill, she turned to The Monkey King for help and made a pledge to have him as my godfather when I got well. Soon I got well and ever since that day, I was regard as the godchild of the Monkey King. Needless to say, I was so proud and so excited to be his godchild. In our neighbourhood there were six to eight Monkey King's godchildren. The parents hosted the Monkey King's Birthday Party in their house in turn. We all dressed up as little monkeys and enjoyed all the great party games and the delicious party food. Those were fancy party days! We had no Halloweens but we had the Monkey King Birthday! (This incident also appeared in page 45)

I am going to devote 6 chapters translation of the birth of this Celestial Monkey King. To me, I think this is the best part of the novel. The Monkey King is not perfect. Sometimes he is careless and very often greedy and weak. Occasionally he becomes bad tempered. He is not born a sage. He is only born a four foot tall little stone monkey. He has all the human weakness and is full of monkey tricks. Chapter by chapter, we read that he learns his lesson the hard way and gains his experiences and gathers momentum year after year. He is mighty but there is always the almighty Buddha. The imprisonment under the Five Finger Mount is his final chance to repent. At last he accepts his punishment and escorts the Holy Monk to India, going through 82 calamities to get the True Buddhist Scripture. It took him 12 (13) years to accomplish this difficult assignment. In the end, he becomes a Happy Junior Buddha, a well earned and well deserved title.

Excerpts from The Journey to the West

Chapter 1 Birth of the Stone Monkey

In the beginning, the Universe was in darkness and chaos. After 129,600 years, the creative force came into being and brought forth day and night: sun, moon and stars, heaven and earth and all living things. After thousands and millions of years, in the midst of a great ocean, there rose an island with a magnificent mountain. It was called the Flower-Fruit Mount. At the top of the Mount, perched an immortal stone, with a magic stone egg inside. Fertilised by the grace of Heaven, sunshine and moonlight, on one fine day, an extraordinary stone monkey was hatched from the egg.

This little Monkey was irrepressible, indestructible, extremely clever and full of mischief. He was so active and energetic that he always enjoyed wandering around the picturesque scenery, and almost non-stop feasting on the luxurious vegetations in his birth place, The Flower and Fruit Mount. In this paradise, he climbed, ate, leapt, jumped, ran, played and made friends with all the other animals especially a colony of monkeys. One day they came to a Great Curtain of Waterfall. Stone Monkey braved the hazardous current and to demonstrate his remarkable courage, he jumped in and out, and jumped in again in front of other monkeys. Behind this big waterfall, he discovered a cave and named it The Water Curtain Cave. There was a splendid and spacious stone mansion inside the Cave, ideal sentry for the whole monkey colony to breed. He led the monkeys inside the Cave; established a Monkey-Court in their new found Residence and was elected King of the monkey clan. From that moment, the Stone Monkey threw away the word Stone in his name. He was crowned and assumed the title, Handsome Monkey King.

The Monkey King appointed a large Courtiers from his flock of monkeys, gibbons and baboons. Everyday they toured the island; gathered fruits and nuts to eat and by night they returned to the West Curtain Cave. The tigers, panthers and wolves were his friends; the deer, rabbits and foxes were his companion. In perfect harmony and concord, the Monkey King enjoyed his happy existence in his little kingdom for four to five hundred years. Until one day, he realised that sooner or later he would grow old and weak. He would have to surrender to the summon of the King of Death. Our Monkey was a fighter and would never just sit back and wait to die. From that day on, his heart was set on searching immortality. He sought everywhere, towns and cities, land and ocean, far and wide, high and low. Ten years went by, at last, he found his Immortal Taoist Master who appreciated his sincerity, took him in and gave him a name, Sun Wu Kung. 孫悟空. The Stone Monkey was delighted with his new name.

Chapter2 The Immortal Master and his Obedient Student

Every day Monkey King learned immortality in great earnest with the Master. He was obedient and diligent, not just in learning, but humbly carried out daily chores in good humour. He did gardening; carried water from the stream, cooking in the kitchen; sweeping the ground etc. The Master was pleased with his new student's buoyant attitude to learn and to work. He gave special attention and taught the monkey all kind of illusion, tricks, magic, yoga, martial art, meditation, transformation into seventy-two different images and forms; the ability to travel 108,000. miles at one single somersault on top of a small cloud. The Master was very glad at his remarkable progress. After another ten years, one day, the Master told him that there was a good reason and he had to leave and return to his homeland at once. Monkey King obeyed and left reluctantly with no question.

Now he could travel fast and was back to Waterfall Cave in no time. During his absence, a Monster invaded his kingdom and enslaved all his subjects to serve him. Monkey King was furious. Using the magical power he learned from his Master, he multiplied himself into a few hundred little monkeys and slain the Monster. This was the first glorious victory in his long list of triumph over numerous monsters and demons. Now the Monkey King resumed his authority and lived peacefully and happily in his kingdom with the little monkeys.

Chapter 3 The Havoc in Dragon Palace (East Ocean) and Hell

It was not long before the Monkey King became mischievous and got himself into big trouble. He went to a city and stole thousands and thousands of weapons to train his subjects to become proper monkey soldiers. Then he realised these weapons were not good enough for him. An Old Monkey told him that he could go to the Palace of the East Ocean Dragon King to try his luck. At once the fearless Monkey dived to the bottom of the ocean and approached the Dragon King, in demand for the celestial weapon of the deep. After a hot argument and confrontation, the Old King was not his match but had to give him the Magic Needle of the Ocean Floor. Knowing the Dragon had three brothers, the Dragon Kings of South, West and North, The Monkey King asked for the precious gold metal armour and the priceless strong helmet from them. By force and by bullying, he obtained the best celestial armour and helmet to clad himself in style. Leaving the angry Dragon Brothers behind, the monkey jumped out from the ocean in his glittering gold outfit and showed off proudly to his subjects. His newly acquired weapon was a magic iron cudgel. He could conveniently turn it into a small needle and store it in his monkey ear.

Very shortly, the Monkey King challenged the Authority of Hell. He stormed into Hell, flashing around his celestial cudgel and threatened the King of Hell to spare his and his followers mortal life so that they could all enjoy eternity. His undaunted spirit brought him in and out from hell and successfully destroyed the Record Book of Life and Death. It seemed to us it was a dream, but it was a real showdown. This big offender of Earth, Ocean and Hell had definitely gone too far. Very soon he has got himself into the top of the wanted list of the heavenly Authority. All the injured party went to Heaven to send in their complains about this wild and irrepressible Monkey. At first, Emperor Jade of Heaven was furious but after a careful discussion with his royal advisers in his Imperial Court, they arrived at a peaceful solution. A special messenger, The Grand White Gold Star old Man carried the Appointment Letter to the Flower and Fruit Mount to see the monkey King. He was offered a post to become the Master of the Horse to God. The good nature of the Monkey King was simple and straight forward. He was easy to please. Delighted to be honoured by this Celestial Title, even though he did not understand what the title meant. He accepted the offer and was escorted to Heaven by the good Old Man to report to duty.

Chapter 4 A Great Revolt in Heaven

However, after a few days, he found out that he was given a very low position as a stable keeper and was jeered all over the heavenly court. Enraged, he revolted and fought his way home to his little kingdom on earth. Again he resumed his carefree and happy life.

The heavenly gods would not leave him alone. Huge Heavenly armies were despatched. Leading by the most fierce General, Heavenly King of The Pagoda Carrier with many brave deities, a fierce battle was engaged. In the battlefield of Fruit and Flower Mount. The Monkey King fought heroically and defeated them one by one, including the god of Might and Wit and the Third Prince La Jar. The Four Heavenly Kings. The army fled back in humiliation. Again, they sent the same Good Old Messenger with much better terms to invite him to Heaven. The Monkey King was allowed to keep his newly acquired Title of Honour, 'The Great Heavenly Sage. He was given a big new mansion with a tall banner flying on top of the roof bearing his Grand New Title; he was given two officials as his staff with many attendants;two buckets of the best wine and ten beautiful gold flowers. The Monkey King had great confidence in his old friend and the terms were good. He accepted the post happily and went back to Heaven to 'Work' for the second time.

Chapter 5 Disrupts Peach Party and Steals Golden Elixirs

His new post was in charge of a team of gardeners who worked in this huge Eternal Peach Garden. The ripe peaches were meant for the Birthday Party of the Heaven Queen Mother Birthday Party. They are big and pink, sweet and juice. Instead of guarding these Immortality Peaches, the naughty monkey stole and devoured all the ripe ones At the same time, when he found out he was not invited to her party, he sneaked into the Queen's Palace; drank her best wine and drunkenly messed the Party Hall. On his way out, he lost his way and came across Lao Tze's Celestial Palace. As he walked in and saw no body around, he helped himself to the Golden Elixirs.

All these devious deeds were unforgivable. This time, he knew he had gone too far but unrepentantly, he fled back to his Home-Cave for sentry.

Subsequently, the infuriated Jade Emperor mobilised a very large army to catch this Horror of Heaven and Earth. With one hundred thousand heavenly soldiers and a very strong team of warrior gods, both side fought dauntlessly. Battle after battle, still no result and still the Monkey ran wild. The Heavenly Army managed to catch all his allies, the wild beasts and monsters in the Island. The monkeys hid inside the Water Curtain Cave and was saved. Everyday they fought from morn till night. The poor Deities were frustrated and humiliated. They turned to Goddess of Mercy for help

Chapter 6 Buddha Imprisoned the Monkey in The Mount of Five Fingers

Eventually, the Goddess of Mercy sent her very able General, True and Fair Second Knight and with the aid of Grand Old Master Lao Tze, they captured the Monkey. He was sentenced to capital punishment. However, as he was immortal. no execution could be inflicted on him. Grand Old Master tried to incinerate him in his furnace where he refined his pills of immortality. After 49 days, instead of killing the monkey, the fire and smoke only added a pair of fiery golden crystal eyes that enabled him to see through things that others could not. He jumped out of the furnace and fought his way home again. At his wits end, the Jade Emperor asked Buddha for help. Buddha was merciful. He did not believe in using force. He gave the monkey a good lecture and made a wager with him. The monkey was very proud of his 'long jump' but he was challenged to jump out of Buddha's lotus-leaf shape Palm. Of course the monkey failed his bet and was imprisoned by Buddha who moved a great mountain, The Mount of Five Fingers on top of him. He survived the weight and pressure but could not move. Buddha told him that he would have to serve his time under the mountain for 500 years; until one day a Tang Monk would rescue him. Then the Monkey would be this Holy Monk's chief disciples. Together with two more disciples, their mission would be hazardous. While escorting the Monk to India, to fetch the True Scriptures of Buddha back to China, he would have to earn his merits in this dangerous journey. He would be rewarded with the most esteemed honour, being made a Junior Buddha.

Chapter 9-12 Chan Yuen Chong The Tang Monk (596-664)

In the 13th year of Emperor Tang Tai Zhong, an Imperial Examination took place at the Tang Dynasty Capital, Changan. A brilliant scholar, Chan Kwong Ju, sat for the Exam, and came first.

The Emperor appointed him to be the High Commissioner of Kwong Zhau down south. He left the capital and took with him his mother and his newly wed wife, daughter of the Prime Minister. Half way, they stayed in a hotel and bought a very big glittering gold fish for dinner. Chan was a very kind man. He took pity on this beautiful fish. Instead of cooking and eating it, he put it back into the river. They continued their journey and met disaster by the river. Two greedy and wicked boatmen killed Chan and their servants. Their bodies were thrown into the river. Chan's wife was very pretty and pregnant. One of the boatmen, Lau Hung, raped her and made her his wife. He also stole all Chan's identity. to report to duty at the Commissioner's Office as an impostor.

Chan's body sank to the bottom of the Ocean. The Dragon King of the ocean was once caught and nearly slaughtered, recognised that Chan was the one who released him back into the river. He repaid Chan by putting his body away with a Eternal Life Pearl into his mouth so that he was only sleeping in his palace. The Dragon King would wait for the right day to come then he would release him back to Earth.

Chan's wife was a very beautiful woman and was well treated by this murderous impostor. When the baby was born, the mother pricked her finger and wrote a letter with blood explaining who he was. She put him in the river on top of a piece of wood. Drifting downstream, the baby was picked up by the Abbot of Gold Hill Temple. The Abbot kept the letter and the baby was given sanctuary in the Temple. Having been a child of prodigious intelligence, he developed a deep interest in the study of Buddhist scriptures. At the age of 18, he undertook the Buddhist vow, shaved his head and received a religious name, Monk Chan Yuen Cheong. Then the Abbot told him about the letter and the murderous horror that happened to his parents 18 years ago. Upon learning the truth, he swore for revenge. With the permission of the Abbot, he set out to look for his mother and his grandparents. One by one, he found them all. Monk Chan told his Grandfather the tragedy in tears and in anger. The heart broken Prime Minister pleaded with the Emperor to send a large army to bring this bloody villain to justice. The enraged Emperor gave the Prime Minister a troop of 30,000 Imperial

Guards, the best soldiers in the Kingdom. Within days the Murderers and Impostors were caught and were executed. The sleeping Father Chan was woken up by the Dragon King and was sent ashore by him. It was a great happy family reunion. He resumed his official duty. The grandparents lived to a happy old age. The pretty Lady Chan peacefully and quietly committed suicide as all decent and virtuous ladies would do in China. Our young Monk determined to stay in the Buddhist Temple offering himself to Buddha and devoting all his time to study the Buddhist's Scripture.

One day the Goddess of Mercy descended to the city with her attendants looking for a qualified candidate to go to the West They were disguised as two filthy priests and gave a lecture to the Young Monk. Physically they were revolting. Yet, her lecture was supreme. She explained to him that the existing Buddhist text, would bring you peace and happiness in this world but The Great Buddha's Text, Nirvana Sutra, would impart Eternal Bliss. All the time Chan Monk was humble and attentive. He was enlightened by the Goddess and was willing and ready to go to India to bring back the Sovereign Buddha Scripture, Nirvana Sutra.

Subsequently, Emperor Tang appointed him as the Holy Monk to travel West to bring back the Great Scripture. Two more monks accompanied him This pilgrimage was again blessed by the Goddess of Mercy. She appeared in her full glory in the sky in front of the Royal Court and the crowd, reinstalled their religious faith to its climax. She equipped the Young Monk with a sacred ceremonial robe and an astral nine rings staff. The Emperor bestowed to him the honourable title, Imperial Royal Brother, a white horse and a purple gold alms bowl.

Chapter 13 The First Calamity

In a cool Autumn morning, the Emperor, with his entire Court, say Good bye to the monks at the City Gate At last these three young monks started their epic and hazardous journey to the west with profound faith and courage. In the beginning, they had a smooth journey, During the first four days, they passed city after city, getting near to the frontier. The local officials welcomed these royal guests and provided them with delicious vegetarian meals and nice rooms to sleep. It was getting near late autumn and the landscape gradually changed from flat land to mountainous region. One early morning, they started before dawn. In the dark, men and horse fell into a trap. Out jumped fifty to sixty demons. They tied them up and brought them back to their Monster King. Two more monsters arrived. Together they feasted on the two monks and would eat the frighten Tang Monk for a later day.

At this terrifying moment, an old man appeared from nowhere. He showed the monk his way out taking with him his white horse carrying all his documents and luggage. The old man told him he had fallen in the Den of Tigers and the two guests, one was a Wild Bull and the other one was a wild Bear. When they reached safety, the old man left in a whirl of gentle breeze riding on a red crown white crane. A note drifted down and it said,

I am the Grand White Star from West Heaven;
My mission is to rescue you from Disasters.
Soldier on, we will give you the protection you deserve.
No need to moan and groan at the Calamites ahead!

Tang Monk fell on his knees to thank the Deity from Heaven. With faith and courage, the lonely soul continued the journey and braved the adversities ahead. Climbing half way up the mountain, he found himself in the midst of tigers, snakes, all kinds of wild beasts and poisonous insects. At this perilous moment, a very famous local hunter, Lau Pak Yan came to his rescue. Effortlessly he got rid of all these wild creatures.

He took Tang Monk home to meet his family, a wife and a widow-mother. Tang Monk said Mass for his dead father. Next day, the parent appeared in their dreams to inform them that because of the Grand Mass, he would be reborn into a rich family in the fertile land of China. After two days, Tan Monk left the grateful family and continued his pilgrimage. The path ahead was treacherous. The worried Monk turned to Lau for help but they had come to the boundary of China and the Tartar country. Lau was not allowed to cross the Boundary Front and had to turn back. As he was leaving, suddenly they heard a monkey yelling from the foot of the mountain, "My Master is coming! My Master is coming!"

Chapter 14 Tang Monk Takes a Loyal Disciple

They found a tiny monkey, buried under the mountain with a tiny filthy monkey head sticking out from the crack of the rock waving his arm up and down. It sounded like thunder but the thundering voice was full of earnest and very impatient. Tang Monk stepped forward, cleaned the weeds and nettles from his dirty face. This was the Monkey King who was assigned to escort Tang Monk by Buddha. In order to release him, Tang Monk was instructed to peel away the Gold Seal at the mountain top. Out jumped the Monkey King to freedom. He knelt down, kow kau four times to pay the highest respect to his new Master. Tang Monk named him, Messenger Sun. Then the hunter knew the Monk was in good hands. He said goodbye and left. The first thing the Messenger did was effortlessly killing a tiger in one blow of his cudgel. He skinned the beast to make himself a dress to cover up his naked body. The Monk was greatly impressed. Their first stop was at a ranch. At the first sight of the Monkey King, an old man refused and afraid to open the door for them. Tang Monk explained to them that the Monkey was his obedient disciple and he himself was the chosen monk by the Emperor to go to India to fetch the true scripture back to China. Upon hearing these, the old man invited them inside and gave them a good vegetarian meal and a hot bath before going to bed. Next morning, after a good breakfast, they left.

Now it was early winter. The pilgrimage treaded along the pretty wintry scenery quietly. Suddenly, jumped out from the bush, six fierce robbers with all sort of lethal weapons flashing at them. The Monkey tried to be civilized and asked them to leave. These brutal robbers instead of retreat, started to attack the Monkey. With one stroke of his magic cudgel, the Monkey killed them all. The kind Monk was horrified. He lectured the Monkey again and again. The bad temper Monkey had more than enough. One somersault, he left Tang Monk and travelled away thousands miles East. He dropped in to have tea with his friend East Dragon King in the Ocean Palace. The Dragon King successfully persuaded him to go back to his Master. On the way back, the Monkey met the Goddess of Mercy. She was glad to see him to rejoin the Monk.

In the meantime, the Goddess of Mercy gave Tang Monk a cotton robe and a pretty little hat trimmed with gold flowers. She taught the Monk a Prayer of Hearty Discipline. With the magic hat and this little prayer, he would be able to tame the Monkey and make him to behave. This magic hat would respond to the prayer and would give the Monkey an unbearable headache, so as to keep him under control. The hat would stick in the monkey head permanently. When the monkey returned, he was given the nice robe and the pretty hat. Without any suspicion, the Monkey put them on. Tang Monk said the little prayer. At once the poor Monkey was in great agony. As the prayer stopped, the pain stopped. Then he realised it was the idea of the Goddess of Mercy. He was furious but there was no escape. No matter how rebellious he was, the little prayer controlled over him. He could never take down the hat himself. As long as he obeyed the Holy Monk, he would be a pain-free Monkey.

Summary

Many thousands years ago, a celestial monkey was born out of a stone egg in the Flowers and Fruits Mountain. After many exciting and mischievous adventures, this irrepressible and extremely clever little monkey got himself into troubles with Heaven, Hell and the Four Dragons Ocean Palaces. Eventually, Buddha and Goddess of Mercy overpower him and assign him a mission to accompany Monk Tang, Tripitaka, to the West to bring back the Sovereign Buddha Scripture, NIRVANA SUTRA. On his way, Monk Tang collects two more loyal disciples and a white horse to help him to face this hazardous journey. It takes them twelve (thirteen) years and encounters 82 calamities. They conquer, they subdue, they convert and they kill countless demons, monsters and evil spirits. Finally, mission accomplish and all become a Junior Buddha and live a celestial life happily ever after!

J. R. R. Tolkien- the author of the The Hobbit: (Lord of the Ring)

Born 03-01-18921973 (aged 81) *The Hobbit* is a fantasy novel written by John Ronald Reuel Tolkien. In the late 1920s, when he was the Professor of Anglo-Saxon at Pembroke College Oxford, he began *The Hobbit* and by January 1933 had finished the story. The first edition of *The Hobbit* was on September 21, 1937 to a wide acclaim

The chief Characters in The Hobbit: (Lord of the Ring):

1. Bilbo Baggins, a respectable, comfort-loving, middle-aged hobbit.

2. Gandalf, a wizard who introduces Bilbo to a company of thirteen dwarves and then disappears and reappears at key points in the story.

3. Gollum, a mysterious creature inhabiting an underground lake; Beorn, a man who can assume bear-form.

4. Bard the Bowman, a heroic archer of Lake-town. They seek
    gold, get it and return home very rich.

The plot involves a host of other characters of varying importance,
such as the twelve other dwarves of the company; elves; men (humans);
trolls; goblins; giant spiders; eagles; Wargs (evil wolves); Elrond the
sage.

The Hobbit and the Monkey King involve a large host of good
and evil characters, countless magical settings and uninterrupted
fantasyland. The big difference of the two is the Hobbit goes for gold
and the Monk King goes for the Buddha Scripture.

CHAPTER 10

Red Chamber Dream
2nd Great Chinese Classical Novels By Cao Sueh
Chin

*Statue of A Great Writer Cao Xueqin
(Cao Sueh Chin) Beijing 1724?-1763?*

Foreword

Red Chamber Dream (also known as The Story of the Stone) written by Cao Sueh Chin, is regarded by many that it is the best romantic novel ever written in Chinese Literature. The background of this novel is 18th Century China. The main theme of this book is a love story with a tragic ending, also about the decline of two powerful wealthy aristocratic households in Peking, involving three young teen age cousins, namely Master Jia Bao (Pao) Yu, a spoil brat; Cousin Lin Tai Yu a pretty but very delicate orphan girl and Cousin Xue Bao Chai a, worldly and wealthy maiden. Bao Yu is in love with Cousin Tai Yu. The family arrange Cousin Bao Chai to marry Bao Yu. Cousin Tai Yu died of broken heart. Master Bao Yu is also heart broken and years later becomes a monk. Before he disappears into the thin air forever, he leaves the family a son, an intellectual heir! The Author presents to us two Jia Dukes, Senior Brothers Duke Ling and younger brother Duke Wing. Loaded with Imperial favor and amassed great wealth by their ancestors, each of them has a very large family with many immediate descendants to enjoy the fruits of the ancestral success. They live side by side in their great Mansions with hundreds servants and maids. In the beginning of the novel, all members of the households, the well-fed and idle ladies and masters, enjoy the luxury, prosperity and comfort with their maids and servants; most of them are frightfully devoted. They live and enjoy themselves in this lavish environment just like most of the privileged class in China. Most days they indulge themselves loitering around, and writing, having parties under the full moon or new moon; serving by numerous maids and servants, visiting each other in their little private splendid reading quarters, go in and out of their private-family temple and having tea and enjoying all the small talks with their special nun-friend; watching and listening opera at their private opera house; chanting and composing poems, cracking jokes and riddles at the family banquet; mocking and flattering to one another; quarrelling over a storm in a tea-cup; burying fallen flower pedals and shedding tears over them; gossiping and grieving over nothing.

Many chapters involve the young cousins' delicate sentiments, telling us their petty joy and their petty sorrow; their self-pity wimps; detail descriptions of the bickering and fighting of the numerous young maids and servants to win favour from their masters and misses. Some commit suicide over disappointment in love and some ill treated by their mistress. The vanity and frustration of all their boring and idle days are happened inside the Grand View Park, an extremely splendid park studded with lakes, streams, many stylish buildings, little mansions, countless shrubs, trees and flowers. Our young master Bo Yu and all the pretty young ladies live inside this Park. This theme Park is built for the 'Welcome Home Imperial Visit,' to honor and to entertain Jia Yuen Chung, their eldest daughter. She is brilliant in her literary achievement. After going through many written tests and conduct tests, she is selected by the Imperial Palace and becomes one of the Emperor's Consort, Royal Concubine Yuen. Every now and then, these palace-caged ladies are allowed to go home to visit their families, providing they go home to a secured, spacious and suitable place. The Jia family spent a huge fortune to built this most famous Grand View Park to welcome her One Day visit. The Imperial Guest is deeply impressed but more than three times, she sighs and advises them should not be too extravagant. The lavishing entertainments take place in this Park. Many happy events happen in this ecstatic environment and all the sad tales also occur in this picturesque Park. Some say that Bao Yu is the self portrait of the author and Grand View Park is the duplicate of Cao's family Park. That is why the Park is so real and the description is so true to life and impressive.

The second motif of the novel is about the Old Revered Lady, Princess Ancestress, Grandma Jia of Bao Yuk. She is the pillar of the family. Her love to the family is acceptance and forgiveness to all her off springs. She is always optimistic, kind, humorous and held the family together through her charismas. Bao Yu is the apple of the eyes of Old Grandma. She adores and spoils him thoroughly. When Bao Yuk is in trouble with his ruthless father, no one can save him but her, his dearest Old Grandma. She is also very practical and takes no nonsense. In choosing a wife for Bao Yu, she goes for brain and health rather than just brain and beauty.

Meanwhile, calamities fall on the family. Properties are confiscated for committing crime of corruption and conspiring with local officials. This 88 years old dowager calms the family and shares out her savings to keep the clan going.

Granny Lau, an old peasant woman is their poor distant relative. She meets all the beautiful people in Grand View Park and is in complete loss. She might be poor but she is very pleasant and genuine. Grandma Jia is kind to her, showers her with presents and makes her feel comfortable.

At the first and the last chapters, a Monk and a Priest appear, and preach some Chinese Religious Philosophy. These mythical and supernatural elements come in to all four great novels! Bao Yu is a left-over repairing stone by goddess Nu Wa Shi and Tai Yuk is a delicate pretty little flower growing next to the stone. They both incarnate at the same time as cousins. At his birth, he carries a piece of precious jade-stone in his mouth All these imaginary nonsense give people a strong belief of fate and strengthen their thought to accept reality which is what they call destiny. More than once, the evil spirits cause big agony and great disturbance to the Grand View Park residents. Every time, the Void Void Priest and the Monk appeared from nowhere and cured them. After all, this is the trend and style of writings in those days. Taoism has its share of performance in all Four Great Chinese Classical Novels. A large percentage of Cao's novel, Red Chamber, is his autobiography. Like most successful writers, he exaggerates and he allows his imagination go beyond this world. We admire his work! We appreciate his writings! We forgive his supernatural and superstitious follies. Thanks to him, we wander amazingly into the wonderland with the true historical value and the real detail daily life of the lords and ladies and also at a gleams of the Imperial Palaces of the Qing Dynasty.

We get so very close to the over indulge and privileged families and in detail into the life of the noble class and the life of their servants and their maids, the working class. I read this novel at my early teen. Right from the beginning, I reject those idle rich and despise on those wimpy characters. I find the plots are very trivial. Yet I was thoroughly absorbed by the magnificent settings. Cao has definitely opened the door for me to walk into the Grand View Park, guiding me to a most enjoyable sight seeing Tour.

In Chapter 82, our delicate and ill-health Tai Yu has a nightmare. In her bad dream, she is forced to leave Grand View Park to marry a widower. In this dream, she dreams her teacher is going to escort her back to Nanking. Vaguely, she thinks she saw her father who wants to take her home. In tears, she begs and begs Grandma to let her stay. and the aunties were there but nobody listen. In a trance, she turns to Bao Yu who kills himself by opening his heart to prove his true love to her. This horrifying nightmare is a very bad omen for our young lovers.

This little verse expressing the moody-lost soul of the author
It seems all pages talking nonsense
but is written with sorrowful tears!,
All might say the author is mad
but who could understand his true sensibilities!
(This is in the first chapter of The Dream of Red Chamber by Cao Sueh Chin)

Cao skillfully sketches 'The Dreams', the wilful and wanton Bao Yu, 'The twelve pretty maids, a rebellious and bad temper servant, the old funny peasant woman, many other young maid-servants; the Revered Grandma Jia and many cousins, aunties and Uncles. He writes page after page of their background and describes vivid pictures of their daily activities and their complex behavior. Thanks to him, after three hundred years, we are able to see, to observe, to learn and to appreciate the true reality in those noble houses during the era of the Qing Dynasty. To Cao, it is just like writing his memoir or diary. He is one of them! He adds in some fairy tales, very strong sense of Taoism, some streaks of mystery to please the multitude. The exaggerations of all those divine happenings satisfy Chinese people's Taoist religious concepts. After all, this is the trend and style of writings in those days. People believe a large percentage of his novel is his autobiography.

The author comes from the same wealthy and powerful family background as the Jia. In 1727, the Caos are charged with the crime of corruption, and fall into disgrace. Their estates are confiscated. The family falls from riches to rags. In spite of Cao's great talent, he failed all his Literary Examinations and is barred from office. It is in these poverty-stricken circumstances that he starts writing this novel. There is hardly any longer and better vivid detail-description of noble house than this masterpiece of his. He is a good painter and has a circle of friends to wine, to talk, to compose poetry and be merry. Sadly these friends are also poor themselves and they can hardly help him out financially. In the cold winter of 1763 (1762) Cao's only son died. Overwhelming with sorrow, the heart broken father died in the same year, without having finishes his novel. He has written 80 chapters. The rest of the novel, another 40 chapters, is finished by a brilliant and successful scholar, Ko Yuok. He finishes writing Cao's novel in the year 1791, 28 years after the death of Cao Hsueh Chin. In 1794, Ko comes first of the Imperial Examination and is appointed to be the Imperial Secretaries of the Inner Office.

If you do not like to read long novels, or you do not have the time, then just looking at these Introduction, Commentary and Excerpts-summaries will be good enough for you to have some idea about the Red Chamber Dreams. I have chosen Chapter 18 The Visit of the Emperor's Consort to her family in Grand View Park. It is a delicate page of a case history. From this Chapter, we have an intimate close look at The 'Rise' of this noble family.

Red Chamber Dream has 120 chapters, the longest of the 4 great novels. It tells no heroic deeds but is regarded by many as the greatest Chinese imaginative narrative. It is mainly full of the trivial matters about the two Dukes' households with a tragic ending love story, entwined three young cousins. Some say that it is mostly read by ladies.

Excerpts + Summaries from Red Chamber Dream-

Here I choose three events to translate and summarize:
1. The Home Visit of the Imperial Consort – Chapter 16, 18, 95
2. The Uninvited Guest, Granny Lau Chapter 6, 39, 40, 41
3. The Three Death Chapter 32, 63, 66, 69, 98,103, 110, 111, 112, 114.

Chapter 18 Imperial Visit

To-day is Duke Jia Cheng's birthday. The two families gather together to celebrate, feasting and watching opera at their great mansion. Suddenly the Chief Urchin Har Bing Chung from Six Palaces arrives with a Decree from the Emperor. At once they stop the Birthday Party, open the Central Gate and burnt incense on a table to receive the Imperial Message at the Central Hall. With a beaming smile, the Chief Urchin sends them a verbal message that by special order of the Emperor, Duke Jia Cheng is to present himself to the Respectful Arrival Palace at once. It turns out to be a happy occasion. Their daughter, Lady Yuen, has been selected to become an Imperial Consort. At an early age, Jia Yuen Chun, the eldest daughter of Jia Clen serves as a Lady Officer in the Imperial Palace. She is brilliant in her literary achievement and has passed the Conduct Excellence Test Now she is selected as the Chief Lady Officer of the Phoenix Palace with the title Praiseworthy and Virtuous Consort!

All the title members of the two Dukes, men and women, have to present themselves in their ceremonial robes to offer thanks to the Emperor. Four large sedans carry The Dowager, the Mother and two Aunties. The retinue is escorted by her grandsons and sons with a large team of servants. The two households are filled with joy and pride. This Imperial favour leads to the climax of Duke Jia's power in Court.

In summer, a decree from the Imperial Palace arrives, stating that the Imperial ladies are granted to visit their parents and family, provided they have adequate and safe accommodation at home for the reception.

115

Consort Jia is allowed to come home for a day on the 15th of the First Moon, The Lantern Festival.

It is a very exciting news. At once the two families work feverishly to build, to repair, to construct, to assemble, to demolish, to design and to plant. Moved all the gates and allies, they plan to join the two Mansions of the Dukes into one and build The Grand View Garden in between. Duke Chen appointed his able nephews Jia Chen and Jia Lien to be in charge. Working under them, they have a large team of stewards, builders, craftsmen, gardeners, workers, blacksmiths, goldsmiths, and carpenters They employ a superb old landscape-architect, known as Man of the Wild Hill. He demolishes many walls, pavilions and servants quarters. Many artifical Mountains, lakes and new pavilions are constructed by him. Beautiful flowers, rare plants and rocks, bamboo and trees are planted according to his plan. Endless supplies come in and huge sum of silverspend. Jia Qiang with the Head Stewed Lai Dai goes to Gu Su to employ opera instructors and before long, they have bought and taken home 12 young girls for their Opera House and 12 young nuns for their new convent. Very soon these young actresses would be well trained and well rehearsed for their performances. The young nuns and priestesses should be able to say their prayers and conduct the religious rituals properly. Five months has gone by. Now it is the 8th of the 1st Moon. The Imperial Palace send the inspector-eunuchs to make sure the rooms and places are comfortable enough for Consort Jia; the security –eunuchs come to inspect and post the security-guards where they think is necessary: the Master of ceremonial eunuchs come to give detail instruction to the whole household, teaching them where to go and how to behave on that big day. Public Work come to clean the environment and the Chief Police Inspector of Five Urban Area the Officers of Public come to clear the street from loiterers and bad elements.

On the 15th of the First Moon, the big day arrives. Nobody has slept a wink that night. Before dawn, in great excitement, all assembles in and out of the Gates, and those with the official titles dressed in the full ceremonial gowns. Waiting and waiting, they wait from morn till late afternoon. They become very tired. Fortunately a eunuch rode to their rescue. He informs them that the Imperial Consort is having a very busy day. By the time she finishes her Dining with the Emperor and Praying to the Buddha, it would be well around seven o'clock for her to start her home visit.

At seven, Her Royal Highness is coming. A long procession of eunuchs carrying dragon banners, Phoenix fans, pheasant plumes and ceremonial insignia. On top of many other beautiful utensils, next comes a yellow umbrella embroidered with seven phoenixes and lots of head-dress and colourful clothing follow. At last her Highness arrives in a gold-top palanquin carried by eight eunuchs. Later she will meet the family inside Grand View Park. Stunning by the elegant magnificence of the Park outside and the dazzling refinement of the decoration inside, she says softly to herself, "This is too extravagant!"

Her Royal Highness starts the tour in a boat in Grand View Park

She starts the tour in a short boat trip. The artificial décor along the Banks and on the water are colourful and even now in mid winter the leaves, flowers and waterfowls looked as real. High and low, beautiful lanterns everywhere creating a glaring crystal world of fantasy. The first stop is going ashore to a marble landing stage. She renames the -Weed Bank' to 'Flowery Harbour' and changes the inscription on the marble archway from 'Immortal Fancy Land' to 'Villa of Reunion' The next stop is arriving at the Temporary Palace While background music playing on both side, the Imperial Consort receives the whole Jia family under the guidance of the Master of Ceremony Eunuch. After the formal ceremony, the Imperial Consort is allowed to have the informal visiting with her close family for a few hours. An Imperial Carriage takes her out of the Park to visit her grandmother, the Dowager, and then her mother, Lady Wang with all the aunts and cousins. The meeting is rather solemn. Instead of chatting and laughing, they are in tear most of the time. The father, uncle and cousins come in to pay their respect and when they redraw, the State Ceremony comes to an end. It is time for her to invite the minor members to see her. Before she is selected by the palace to leave home, she and Pao Yu stay with their Grandmother and are inseparable. When Pao Yu is four, she teaches him to read and write. She loves her little brother dearly. So naturally, now, she asks about Pao Yu and sends for him first. Her father has told her Pao Yu is doing well in his literary composition. When she sees him she holds his hand and is so delighted though in tears again.

Accompanying by all, Consort Jia enters into the Park. After having a sumptuous banquet in the glittering luxurious Main Hall, Consort Jia turns round and says the 2ne time, "This is far too extravagant !

She starts going round the Park and names them one by one. The Park is named The Grand View Park; the Phoenix Alights is changed to Bamboo Lodge; Crimson Fragrance and Green Jade, Iris Court; Apricot Tavern Comes Into Sight becomes Hemp Washing Cottage; the main hall is named Grand View Pavilion; the east wing is Variegated Splendour; on the west Fragrance Tower. There are many more names named by her that night. After naming the places, Consort Jia wants each of the boys and girls write an inscription to a given place, followed by a poem. The poems are beautifully written about this magnificent Imperial Visit and the Enchanting Grand View Park. With some help from the girls, Pao Yu has done well too. The Imperial Consort is pleased, especially with her dear brother's hand in. Here is the one she likes best from him:

The Sight of the Apricot Tavern

Looking at yonder is the villa,
At the Apricot Tavern, the Sign flies and welcomes customers.
Geese swim on the caltrop pond.
Amid mulberries and elms, swallows find their nests.
Green leeks ripened in the spring fields.
Within ten miles, the scent of the rice flowers spreading.
In this era of prosperity, there is no hunger and no cold.
There is no need to toil over farming and weaving

Now is Jia Chiang's turn to produce the programmes of the stage plays to entertain the Imperial Consort. His team of 12 young actresses give superb performances. They act enchantingly; they dance divinely and they sing bewitchingly. When they finish their performance, Consort Jia gives nice prizes to the outstanding talented actress Ling Kuan. She praises Ling and thinks she is the best and has a bright future.

When they finish banqueting in Grand View Hall, they walk to a few more places. They come to the Buddhist Convent by the hillside. The inscription given by Consort Jia to this place is, 'Mercy Sailing in the Bitter Sea.' She washes her hands, burns incense and prays to Buddha. She also generously gives the nuns and priestesses many gifts. On behave of the Imperial Consort, the eunuchs distribute to everyone all sorts of presents, such as precious jade, gold, silver, money, silk and satin. The list includes stewards, servants, maids, builders, gardeners, workmen, actresses,cooks and lantern-workers so on and so forth that no one in the two mansions will be left out.

At three o'clock in the morning, time to say good-bye. Before the departure, the Imperial Consort in tears, for the third time, tells them, not to be so extravagant!

Chapter 6 The Uninvited Guest-Granny Lau

Granny Lau is a humble peasant woman who lives with her daughter and son-in-law in a village She helps her daughter to look after two grandchildren and the son-in-law is a farmer. One day persuaded by her son-in-law, she goes to the city to pay a visit to the Wing Mansion. Hopefully she can gain some financial help from these wealthy and powerful distant relatives. She takes her four years old grandson to go with her.

She is stunted in awe by the two huge stone-lions and the grandeur at the front of this big mansion. She asks to see Mr. Chau, a steward but it turns out meeting his wife instead. Mrs Chau gives her a warm welcome and makes arrangement for her to see some important members of the household. At first, it is Pink Yee, the head maid and concubine of Jia Lien. She shows them to the inner quarter. Pink Yee dresses in silk and covers in gold and silver ornament. Granny Lau has nearly mistaken her as the Mistress Fung Tsai.

Meanwhile Fung Tsai comes in to have dinner. Ten to twenty serving maids rally around to serve dinner to the Ladyship. All the time Granny Lau is waiting at the corner of another room. She feels rather uncomfortable at these dazzling and luxuriously surrounding. Her waiting is not in vain. After hearing the reason of her visit, Fung Tsai instructs Pink Yee to give Lau twenty teals of silver and a string of coins to take home. Before leaving they are invited to enjoy a sumptuous meal. With ten thousand thanks, Granny Lau and her grandson left by the back gate.

Chapter 39 to 41 Granny Lau Revisits Grand View Park

Granny Lau comes to the Jia Mansion again. She is most grateful for the generous help from the last visit. They have a good harvest this year so she brings with her some fresh farm products to show her gratitude. When Grandma Jia hears about her presence, she invites Lau to her quarters. It is a good meeting. The dowager is pleased to chat with her humorous guest; to hear villages news and to listen to her interesting tales. She is invited to stay for a meal and then to stay over night. They give her a bath and a change of nice clothing. She is having a time of her life.

She is a born entertainer. She tells very funny clean jokes and very interesting tall-stories to humour and to satisfy the curiosity of these leisure gentry. Our hosts mock and make a fool of her around, but our old lady accepts these Fun Challenges in great spirit, leaving Granny Jia and her whole company of people roaring and laughing. Undoubtedly this old peasant woman has successfully provided a very amusing and happy time to all. She enjoys the delicacy and fine wine of this noble house listening to the soft music by their musicians in their music box and occasionally makes comparison such as to the price of one dish equals to the cost of living a whole year at home.

Granny Lau is offered some fried egg-plant. After savouring it slowly, she likes it very and asks for the recipe. They give it to her:-

The Recipe of the Egg-Plant Dish
1. Peel and cut egg-plants into small pieces,
2. Fry with chicken fat.
3. Dice chicken breast, fresh mushrooms, bamboo shoot and dried mushrooms.
4. Add spice bean curd and various kind of preserved fruit.
5. Dice and mix and boil altogether in the chicken soup until dry.
6. Add sesame oil and pickles and store it tightly in a porcelain jar

The old peasant woman marvels at the fine food and drinks and gratefully she returns their kindness with providing the hosts out burst of laughter after laughter. When they have a leisure walk in the park, they come to Green Lattice Nunnery, The eccentric young nun, Miu Yu serves tea to Granny Jia and the others. She entertains everybody in her Tea Party! She is not too happy to have a peasant guest in her nunnery. She makes sure that everything Lau touches will not stay in her presence. She is always arrogant but has a terrible tragic ending. She is kidnapped by some gangster and no one knows where she has gone.

Now is the time for resting. Our granny Lau by mistake loiters into Master Pao's elegant and beautiful bedroom. She sprawls out and sleeps on it. The head maid, Chai Yen, is shocked and gets her out of the situation just in time.

After 3 days and 2 nights, Lau goes home with a cart-load of presents and 108 tael of silver. This tidy sum would be enough for them to buy a small business or acquire some farmland at home. After saying tens and hundreds times of thanks, finally, they escorted Granny Lau to a hired carriage and see her off.

This is not the end of the story of this poor relative with the Rich Chai Family. Years later, calamities fall on the Chai family. They are charged of corruption and manslaughter. Duke Ching has a narrow escape but not his brother's family. The great Jia family has declined ever since and in due course, Granny Lau saves the teenage granddaughter of Grammar Jia from a dreadful marriage. She keeps the girl in her village. Under her protection, the girl is happy and well. She lives a healthy rustic lifestyle in the country which is entirely different from the luxurious Grand View Park.

Chapter 32 The Death of Maid Kim Chuen

Kim Chuen Yee is one of the head maids of Lady Wang. She has been serving her ladyship more than 10 years. She is a young and pretty girl.

One hot summer day, Pao Yu strolls through the Park. and wanders into his mother's quarters. He finds she is having a nap. with her eyes close. The maid Kim is also dozing by her side This wanton and wilful young master starts teasing and flirting with Kim. They exchange some harmless jokes.

At this moment, her Ladyship opens her eyes. She slaps Kim's face and scolds her angrily, calling her shameless slut. Instead of. caution her own son, the culprit, she sends for Kim's family to take her home for good. The poor maid pleads and pleads for forgiveness but Lady Wang keeps on accusing her. Pao Yu has long disappeared from the scene, looking for another playground to amuse himself. Maid Yu Chuen,sister of Kim, has to send for their mother to take her away. After two days, in disgrace and feeling wrongly accused, Kim commits suicide by throwing herself in a well at the east-south corner of Grand View Park This time, Her Ladyship sends for the mother herself. She compensates her 50 teals of Silver, some jewels and some clothing. A High Mass is said for the Decease. Then the Mother has to kowtow and to thank her Ladyship before she leaves the Mansion.

Chapter 63 Death of Jia Ching in Yuen Chin Monastery

The Recluse, Jia Ching grandson of Duke Liang, died of taking over-dose of Taoist drug in the Taoists Temple.

It is another summer day. The Grand View Park young gentry are having a great feast to celebrate Master Pao Yu's birthday. The food is sumptuous, the wine is superb and the party-games and the fun-gambling are exciting. As it is an informal party in Pao Yu' private Chamber, they change into comfortable clothes and let their hair down.

Next day the party continues. While they are scuffling in fun, some servants from Ling Mansion come rushing up in frantic to announce the news of the death of their Old Master Jia Ching, who is a Taoist-Recluse living in the Yuen Ching Monastery. For years, he has been practicing Taoist's Yoga, watching the position of the stars and taking pills of sulphur-mercury. He believes he will become an immortal. Instead he has died of over-taking Taoist drug. The belly of his corpse is hard as iron; his skin turns purple and his lips cracks. Lately he has concocted some heavy formula of Elixir He believes in Elixir and Elixir kills him.

At once Madam Yu, the daughter-in-law, is in charged on her own and sends messengers to inform her husband and her son who are away on Official Errands. She hurriedly orders to have all the Taoists priests lock up and in chain. Finding the Monastery too small and too far from the city, she has the corpse moved into the family temple, the Iron Step Temple. Madam Yu realizes that the weather is too hot and the funeral must not be delayed. She gets an astrologer to choose a day for it. Three days later, the funeral ceremony starts and masses are performed.

When the Emperor hears from The Board of Ceremony, he issues a Decree to give a high honour to the deceased, son of Duke Liang, Jia Doi Far In view of his grandfather's merit, he is to be promoted posthumously to the fifth rank, and moves to the Imperial Kwong Look Temple. All in Court, from princes and dukes downwards are allowed to go to the funeral to offer their condolences. All the ministers at court and all the Jias at home praise and thank the exceeding kindness of the Emperor.

Upon hearing the death of Jia Ching, the son Jia Chen and the grandson Jia Jung hurriedly gallop home. The formal funeral ceremony takes place on the 4th day. At five o'clock in the morning, the cortege is taken from the Temple back to the Main Hall in Ling Mansion where the relatives and guests file in to pay their respect. More than ten thousand people lining along the road to watch, some admire at the splendid funeral procession; some envy and criticize the extravagance. The cortege remains in the Hall for a few days more and then accompanied by the close members of the family, their stewards and servants, is moved back to the Temple. After one hundred days, the coffin will be taken to their ancestral burying ground. That will be his eternal resting place and this is the end of the story of the wealthy Taoist Recluse.

Chapter 97 and 98 In Sorrow Lin Tai Yu Returns to Heaven

Po Yu loses his precious jade. It just simply disappears mysteriously. He turns into a complete idiot and is in coma most of the time. The family try everything to help him get better. Nothing works. Sometimes he is in total coma and sometimes has a sudden relapse becoming deranged. At last the three senior ladies, The Dowager, Lady Wang and Fen Hasi, put their heads together and think out a plan. They presume a wedding might help. As for brides, one end is the wealthy, good temper and healthy Pao Chai; the other end is the poor, ill health and indifferent Tai Yu. All favour Pao Chai even they fully aware that Pao Yu is deeply in love with Tai Yu. To guarantee a smooth wedding, they cover up the truth and no one is allowed to mention who is the bride.

All the time, the poor Tai Yu is very ill, can hardy get out of bed. She feels lonely and spits out blood from her painful chest very often. When she hears Pao Yu and Pao Chai's wedding, she is completely shattered and does not want to live anymore. The three Senior Ladies go to Bamboo Lodge to comfort her and send a doctor to see her. They cannot come often because they have to attend to all the business of the wedding. Grandma, the dowager, loves Tai Yu very much but she loves Bao Yu even more. She thinks it is only right for her to choose a Happy and Healthy Bride for Bao Yu.

On the very day of Pao Yu's wedding, no one comes to see her. She feels lonely and she is very ill. All she asks for is a quick death. One of her chief maids, Seuh Ngan is transferred to attend and to serve

Po Chai on her wedding day. The faithful Zee Kuen is with her. She burns the handkerchiefs with inscriptions and also throws the booklet of her poems into the fire. She dies on Pao Yu's wedding day! Before she takes her last breathe, she spates out blood and screams out loudly, "Pao Yu! Pao Yu! How could you!" As for Bao Yu, he is getting married in the same hour. All the time he thinks he is marrying his true love, Cousin Tai Yu. The Dowager thinks otherwise. She loves Tai Yu dearly but she finds this granddaughter is too delicate, too morbid and too ill to be a healthy bride. The wedding ceremony proceeds smoothly. The bride is carried in a big sedan-chair with the house musicians playing some cheerful notes to accompany the arrival of the bride. The cover-up works until the moment when Pao Yu lifts up the veil of the Bride. When he sees Pao Chai instead of Tai Yu, he is bewildered, deranged and totally confused again. Years later, influenced by his able wife, he stops messing around with young ladies in Grand View Park and takes more seriously in his studies. He produces an heir. He brilliantly comes 7th in the Imperial Examination. But then, he never goes home. He disappears with a Taoist Priest. This is the end of our story.

Summary

In a noble and wealthy family, there are two brothers, Duke Jai Shu and Duke Jia Ching. They inherit their titles from their father. Their mother, Duchess Jia, is loved and respected by all. The brothers live next to each other and have a very large family with over hundred servants. Jia Yuen Chun, the oldest daughter of Duke Jia Ching, is chosen as an Imperial Consort. To honour her home visit, The Jia family build a magnificent garden, namely, Grand View Park. The young teenage Jias and their pretty cousins all move into the Park and live in leisure and in luxury. The son of Duke Ching, Pao Yu is clever but wanton, spoiled by the Dowager. He is in love with Cousin Tai Yuk. But the family arrange Cousin Pao Chai to marry Pao Yu. Poor Tai Yu died of broken heart. Years later Pao Yu disappears and becomes a monk. Before Po Yu left, calamities fall on the family. They are charged of corruption and manslaughter. Duke Ching has a narrow escape. The great Jia family has declined ever since.

William Shakespeare

William Shakespeare (baptised April 26, 1564 – died April 23, 1616) was an English poet, actor and playwright. He was widely regarded as the greatest writer of the English language, as well as one of the greatest in Western literature. He was also a great actor. He was born in Stratford-upon-Avon, Warwickshire, England

Romeo and Juliet, is a tragedy by William Shakespeare about the fate of two young ill-fated lovers. Romeo and Juliet both died, a well known tragedy in the West

It is perhaps the most famous of his plays and is thought to be the most renowned love story in Western history. The play has been highly praised by literary critics for its language and dramatic effect. It was among Shakespeare's most popular plays during his lifetime and, along with Hamlet, is one of his most frequently performed plays. Its influence is still seen today, with the two main characters being widely represented as young lovers with a very tragic ending.

In our Dream of the Red Chamber, our heroine died but her lover lived and with his wife, he gave the family a son. Eventually, he faded into a Dreamland with a Taoist. He was a wanton boy and ended his life as an irresponsible father and husband.

CHAPTER 11

Romance of the Three Kingdoms, 3rd Great Chinese Classic Novel- By Luo Guan Zhong (1330-1400)

A Famous Battle Scene of the Three Kingdoms

Brief Introduction and Comment

'The Romance of the Three Kingdoms' is a historical novel with an astonishing fidelity to history. Many critics say, that Luo's greatest achievement is to blend history with fiction in such a skilful way, people can hardly tell the facts from the made up stories. Ninety per cent of the characters in the novel are real but thirty per cent of the events could be fictitious, exaggerated and dramatised.

The novel involves over one thousand people and approximately three hundred events. Altogether Luo writes and compiles one hundred and twenty chapters, including fifteen very important characters and numerous famous battles and renowned places. The story is long and complex with heroes and villains alike, many have become household names. In the old days, those who could not read and write learnt them from the storytellers, operas and street performers. In the 21st century, many learn from cinema and television. The leaders of the

Three Kingdoms are warlords themselves. After countless battles, nobody achieves a clear win. Near the end of their ruling days, in their own domain, they proclaim themselves emperors, except Cao. This is solid proof that he is a true patriot and never betrayed his country, during the Han Regime. He remained loyal to the Han Emperor as his Prime Minister until his last breadth. He is ambitious but his ambition is for a righteous goal to unite the Han Dynasty and not allow it to be torn apart by warlords. Some historians gave him a fair and favourable judgement. Most of the story tellers, novelists and stage-performers have a habit of presenting the weak and crafty Lau of Shu, as a humble and kind big brother figure but to the true hero and great genius of Cao of Wei, they depict him as a wicked and ugly villain and a scoundrel.

Three Kingdoms with their Rulers
Cao Coa Liu Bei Sun Quan
(AD 155-220) (AD 160-223) (160-250)

1. Cao Cao, ruler of Kingdom Wei (220-265) is the regent for the minor Emperor Xian. He is better known as Prime Minister Cao, and is famous for his terrifying, ruthlessness and as a literary genius. His success depends on his ability rather than family influence. He laughs and smiles very often but rather superficially, without warmth. The Northern part of China is the territory of Wei. He sends his force, the righteous Army, out to crush the traitors and rebels. In the name for the unity of Han Dynasty, as Prime Minister, he acts for the Han Emperor as his regent. He is fighting patriotically for his country and his Emperor. His famous characteristic gesture is laughing and smiling. He is not just a brilliant statesman but is also a very good poet and a romantic artist. In the year A. D. 210, he architects the magnificent Bronze Bird Towers in his homeland County of Ip, above River Zhang. In fact, it is three Towers connected by three bridges. He declares that when his ambitions are fulfilled,the country is united and people live a peaceful and good life, he will retire into his Dream Towers with his favourite beautiful ladies. But ten years before his retirement, this genius and dreamer dies. We admire him because he is a strong and decisive leader and extremely loyal to Han too. Up to his last day, he still calls himself the Loyal Prime Minister of Han. As

well as a courageous warrior he was also a great politician; establishing many farming-militant colonies; building canals and defensive walls. His soldiers obtain hereditary status from him and thus create a new social class of soldiers. In A. D. 220, he died in bed at the age of 66, posthumously Emperor Wu of Wei by his son Cao Pi. Emperor, Wei Wen.

2. Liu Bei, leader of Kingdom of Shu (AD 221-263) in the west of China, comes from a very humble background. Before he joins the army, he sells mats and sandals in the market where he meets two gallant soldiers and become sworn brothers of three, uniting under the famous "Peach Garden Oath." With the same surname Liu, he claims he is the distant relatives of Emperor Xian of Han But who knows if this is true. His virtue is greater than his talent. He assembles able and loyal men to aid him and tries to seek the restoration of the Royal Throne back to the former glory. He seems kind and wins his followers' heart by his benevolence in his speech and his emotional display of his frequent out burst of weeping in front of his generals and adherents. From a very weak force, it becomes stronger with the new recruit, Kong Ming. Gradually, with the help of this new Prime Minister Kong and five courageous generals, nick – named the Five Tiger Generals, Liu acquires a fertile corner of China and proclaims it the Kingdom of Shu. Tragically, his two sworn brothers die before him. In the year 221, Liu calls himself the Emperor of Shu Han. One year later, a very bitter and sorrowful Liu is defeated by General Lu Sun, of Wu and dies shortly in the City of the White Emperor at the age of 63.

3. Sun Quan(160-250) leader of Kingdom Wu (222-280), proclaims himself Emperor Wu Dadi, 220 AD. His father is a Han Grand Warden, a courageous general, joining the Allies to overthrow the traitor Dong Zhuo. By luck, he obtains an ancient Jade Seal, the Imperial Treasure of the Chu Warring State Period. He dies in battle at the age of 37. His eldest son, Sun Char is also a great Warlord but dies young. He is wounded in battle and dies at the age of 26. Sun Quan inherits the throne from his brother at the age of sixteen. Wu is a rich county, within the flat and very fertile Yangtze Delta. The Sun Clan rulers allow their nobles to have large estates of land with a hundred peasants and allowing them to build up their local government. It is the last of the Three Kingdoms to surrender to the new Jin Dynasty.

This long novel can be divided into three sections:

Section # 1. Chapter 1 – 35

The Confederation armies, headed by Cao Cao and Yuan Shao, are successfully crushed, firstly, the over-powerful eunuchs, secondly, the Yellow Scarf Rebellion and then thirdly, the ruthless Grand Officer Dong Cherk. Finally, the alliances get rid of Dong and Cao claims regency over the weak Han Emperor. In this section, the most famous event is The Peach Garden Oath of the three blood brothers.

Section # 2. Chapter 35 – 85

This section is the longest. Countless battles are fought among the Three Kingdoms, but there is no winner. All three sides are faithfully supported by their loyal, farsighted advisers and brave commanders. Ironically, the three leaders of the three Kingdoms, dead or alive, are nominated to be emperors by their courtiers, between AD 215 and 222 The major event in this section is, 'The Battle of the Red Cliff.'

Section # 3. Chapter 86 – 120

This last section has a conclusive ending. An ambitious General of Wei, Sima Yan overthrows the Cao family. It is a peaceful power transition. Sima receives the abdication from Emperor Wei Yuan and becomes the first Jin Emperor. Finally China is united into one Empire AD. 265-420. The major event of this section is Zhu Ge Liang, known as Kong Ming capturing and releasing Meng Huo seven times.

The author has given mythic status to many characters. Obviously, he follows the Taoist tradition and tries to attract great interest of the readers. In one Chapter, Kong Ming is a recluse. In another chapter he is a strategist,in next chapter he is a magician. Many events have been exaggerated by the storytellers to please the audiences. Here I have selected three major episodes for you to experience the behaviour of the ancient Chinese warriors and the historical land and sea battles with the complex mentality of their followers. They truly represent a wealth of fanciful, historical, fictional, most popular dramatic and magical Chinese narrative. Many people think that it ranks next to 'The Journey to the West'

Excerpts + Summaries from the Three Kingdoms

Chapter 1 Three Sworn Brothers and Their First Victory
Chapter 48-49 Sea-Battle of Red Cliff
Chapter 87-90 Seven Defeats of the Barbarian Chief

Chapter One The Peach Garden Oath of Liu, Guan and Zhang

It is in the fourth year of the reign of Emperor Ling, Han Dynasty. This weak Emperor is under the control of the abusive eunuchs who in their power struggle, persecute many officials of integrity and ability. It was a bad year. People suffered pitilessly from many natural disasters, such as earthquakes, hurricanes, tidal waves, landslides, as well as from the corrupted officials. Hungry people steal, rob and revolt against the authority. Of all the organised rebels, The Yellow Scarf is the strongest one. It gathers more than four hundred thousand followers; captures a city; makes banners and proclaims that their leader has received a mandate from 'Heaven,' through 'South China Old Deity' and is given the 'Three Heaven Books. This book has the supernatural power to heal and to kill. The leaders of the Yellow Scarf are Three rRebels Brothers, Zhang Kok,. Zhang Bao, and Zhang Liang They name themselves Heaven General, Earth General, and People's General.

The Emperor and his ministers are desperate to try to crush the rebels. They mobilise force together and also put up public posters to invite people to join the army. Liu Bei, seven foot tall, meets the eight foot tall Zhang Fei, in front of the army barrack. Liu is a penniless hawker. Zhang is a rather wealthy butcher. Driven by patriotism, both come to look at the inducement poster and become friends instantly. Next minute, they sit down for a drink at a wine shop and before long another patriot joins them. His name is Guan Yu. He is a nine foot tall fugitive. They drink, they admire each other, they express their love of their country and their noble intention to join the army. After the drinking party, Zhang Fei invites them to his house. In his peach garden, the beautiful peach trees are in full bloom. The three agree to become sworn brothers taking the oak under the peach trees. It is a very solemn ceremony. Zhang Fei puts up a grand altar using live stocks, white horse, black ox and all the usual ritual. In front of the burning incense, they kneel down and ask Heaven to witness their fidelity and loyalty to each other as true brothers. These three sworn brothers will live as one; work as one; fight as one and die as one. Liu is 28 years old, the eldest of the three. He is Brother #1. Guan, Brother #2, comes second. As Zhang is the youngest, he is Brother #3. Then Zhang slaughters an ox and they have a big feast. Next day they gather as many as five hundred brave young men from the village. They buy battle horses and equip themselves with the best weapons and armour. After a few days, it is report that one of the Yellow Scarf General Cheng Zhi Yuan leads fifty thousand rebels to invade County Zhuo. Ready for war, they march with their small army to see the Grand Warden Liu Yan of County You and his Constable, Zhou Jing. The Grand Warden is very pleased to accept them into the main force. The surname Liu brings the two Lius close to the same family tree as their Imperial Ancestors. The Grand Warden happily calls Bei his nephew which is quite an honour to our new recruit. After a few days, it is report that one of the Yellow Scarf General Cheng Zhi Yuan is leading fifty thousand rebels to invade County Zhuo. Liu Yan gives five hundred soldiers to Zhou and orders the Three Brothers to go along to fight against Rebel Jing. A t the foot of Mount Ta Yu, the two armies meet. A short and fierce fighting follows. In the battle-field, Bei is flanked by his two brothers. The mighty Zhang kills the assistant rebel general with one stroke of his spear and then the valiant Guan cuts the rebel chief commander into two halves. The enemy flees and the battle is over. Many rebels are taken prisoners. The happy General Warden goes out of the city-gate to welcome the triumphant army.

This is the Three Sworn Brothers' first victory. Hundreds and hundreds of big and little battles are to follow. They might win some battles but they never win the War. Of the three brothers, Pei is the last to die in bed with a broken heart at the age of 63. Guan, at the age of 58, is executed by Sun, the King of Wu. At the age of 54, Zhang has a tragic death, murdered by his own generals. Both are beheaded. Up to the last moment of their death, China is still divided into Three Kingdoms, all claiming their legitimacy to the Throne of China. 'The Peach Garden Oath' becomes a legend. Thousands and thousands, especially the underworld and many honest working class people, follow the pattern of the ceremony of 'The Peach Garden Oath' to strengthen the bonds of friendships and brotherhood among themselves.

Even in overseas China Towns, you can often see shops and restaurants with the Shrines of the Three Brothers, tucked away at the corner with offerings. Ironically, another popular place to revere these warriors is the Police Station. In nearly every Police Station in Hong Kong, you can see a neat little altar with the Three Brothers or sometimes only # 2 Brother Guan placed in a bright spot. My husband was a policeman in the auxiliary force, and he is a catholic. But Christian or no Christian and volunteers or no volunteers, he has to follow the tradition. When the new graduates from the Police Academy report to duty, he and his mates in full smart uniform, one by one, have to bow low to the altar to show their respect and to ask for blessings and protection from these legendary heroes!

In 208, Cao Cao marched south with his mighty army hoping to quickly unify the empire but instead he suffered a big defeat. In this famous Red Cliff Sea battle out of a million strong force, only twenty seven cavalry. left to escort him back to Wei, his home country.

A Famous Sea Battle -Red Cliff

Chapter 46-49 The Battle of Red Cliff (190A. D.)
Chapter 46 The Big Feast of Cao Cao

Cao Cao always considers himself the Defender of the Imperial Throne, declaring all the time that he has been fighting most of his life to crush rebels and remove traitors as a loyal subject of Han. Now at the age of fifty-four, with his million strong troops, thousands of civilian and military officers, and an armada, he is ready to subdue Jiang Nan the region of Wu, South of Yangtze River. He has overcome nearly all his enemies except Wu. Cao's ambition to cross the Yangtze River to overpower Wu is just a matter of days now.

On the eve of the week before the Sea Battle, Cao gives a big banquet for his civilian and military staff. The full moon is big and bright. shining over the river, hills, cities and our jubilant Commander Cao is in high spirits. He toasts to his officers, promising them victory, prosperity, peace and high honours. Roused by the startlingly beautiful scene of crows flying and crying over the moon to the south, he composes and sings a beautiful banquet ode.

The main theme of the poem is about a homeless crow. One of Cao's close friends, Grand Warden Liu Fu, comes forward to tell him that this is bad omen. Cao is drunk and in his murderous wrath, he kills Liu with one stroke of his lance. At once, the horrific party is over in horror. Nevertheless, next morning, Cao is sober and full of remorse. He gives a state funeral with soldiers to escort the cortege back to Liu's home town.

Chapter 47 Borrowing Arrows

Sun Quan, 160-250, the ruler of Wu is having a very important meeting with his military officers and advisers to decide whether he should go to war or submit to Cao. After a long discussion, the hawks win. Quan's two able and farsighted commanders, Zhou Yu and Lu Su change the defeatist attitude. Kong Ming, the guest adviser, is behind all this. He rallies and does the ground work to prepare them how to turn the imminent doom to a proud victory. Now they are allies and are supposed to fight against one common enemy. But full of envy, covetousness, treachery and selfishness, in the name of patriotism the courageous commanders of Wu and the astute Prime Minister of Shu set traps and lay tricks behind each other's back. They try to overshadow one another by deceit and dishonesty; they win victory by tricks and fraud. It is vile and atrocious and have badly influenced the virtue of the listeners, the readers and the viewers in China over a thousand years. (It is said that old people should not read 'The Romance of Three kingdoms' because it is too treacherous. Old people should live a quiet and simple life so as to enjoy their golden sunset days in peace and in harmony. After all, in life, the best policy is honesty.

The Northern land soldiers are not used in the naval battle. Cao seeks advice and some of Jiang Dong spies manage to offer a fatal plan to Cao, to link the floating fleet one by one with iron chains because this will provide better stability to his soldiers. This sounds good and

Cao accepts the plan and links his fleet ready for battle. Some of his advisers remind him of fire attack, but Cao knowing well this is not an easterly wind season, dismisses their worries. On the other side Sun prepares one hundred fire boats to attack. Kong Ming is in charge of producing one hundred thousand arrows within three days. He accepts this mission impossible. He borrows twenty swift boats from Lu Su. Each boat is equipped with a thousand bundles of dry straw wrapped in black cloth with thirty soldiers on board. Hong waits and at the third night tremendous fog spreads across the river and the visibility is zero. Hong invites Lu to come along to collect arrows and tells Zhou to have five hundred soldiers on shore ready to transport the arrows back to the camp. At mid-night, the fog is at its thickest. At once Kong orders his soldiers sailing the boats close to Cao's armada, shouting out loud and beating drums to arouse the enemy. Cao sends for ten thousand crossbowmen to counter attack these invisible invaders. The noisy attackers come closer and the ten thousand bowmen shower their arrows like rain towards the hidden enemy. When the sun rises, the fog lifts and the swift boats heavy with arrows, hurry back to Zhou's camp where five hundred soldiers are waiting to collect ten thousand more arrows.

In the mean time, two sides are ready for a big decisive battle, 'The Battle of Red Cliff'. Wei has a million strong land soldiers and Wu has a fifty to sixty thousand valiant navy force. Kong and Chou put their heads together and think of a brilliant strategy. They are going to use fire to destroy the armada. They are waiting for the easterly wind. Legend says Kong borrows Easterly Wind from Heaven. He employs 500 strong soldiers to build an altar with three layers wide and flat platforms; the total height of each layer is three feet; total area is seventy-two feet. Kong also has one hundred and twenty soldiers to surround very close to the altar. The lower layer of the platform is studded with green, red, white and black flags, seven flags for each colour; second layer with sixty yellow flags, placed according to the position of the Eight Trigrams (Ba Gua) four people standing at the top of the altar fully dressed in ceremonial gowns holding a long pole, the Seven Stars Banner, Sword and Incense-burner; and another twenty four men holding all sorts of rites and enchanting articles going round and round the altar Kong goes up to the top altar three times a day, putting on the Taoist gown, with hair down, and feet bare; holding the sword and muttering his prayer. On the third day, after midnight, the Easterly wind blows briskly from the south shore. It works!

Chapter 49 The Burning of the Armada

Once the Easterly wind blows, Wu starts the attack without delay. There are four squadrons. In each squadron, it has twenty Light Fire Boats in front and three hundred large battle–ships follow. The Fire Boats are well stocked with dry straws, dry weeds, materials soaked in fish oil and cinder etc. A double spy, Huang Gai also joins the sea battle. He prepares twenty fire boats with four large warships sailing towards the Chief Commander Cao's colossal flagship. Cao is not on guard, instead he welcomes Huang, thinking he is a friend. In fact double spy Huang turns out to be the first deadly attacker. Disguised with pretentious banners and signals, Huang cheats his way close enough to burn and attack the armada. The large squadrons follow close and instantly set Cao's linking fleet on fire. There is no way for the seven thousand warships to escape. The roaring flame leaps mercilessness from ship to ship. They are all linking together, and face the tragic doom together. Under the strong Easterly Wind, the blazing fire, the killing heat, the screaming, crying and shouting of the soldiers of both sides present a picture of hell! The Red Cliff of Yangtze River is soaked with red blood and the cliffs also turn maroon by the black smoke. The river is filled with dying soldiers, burning bodies and charred corpses. This is indeed the biggest and the most sorrowful Naval Battle in ancient Chinese History! The Commander's Flag Ship is on fire. One of his loyal generals, Zhang Liu, rushes to rescue him in a small light cutter. Cao jumps away from the roaring flames and barely escapes with a few guards. The double spy Huang chases the cutter but is shot down by General Zhang. They land in a safe spot and manage to gather three thousand men to retreat away from the burning armada on the river and the fiery camps on land. This small army, was tired, frightened, and demoralised and many are injured both physically and mentally. They had to face ambush after ambush. Lucky for Cao, he saves his skin and flees back to Wei but out of a million strong force, only twenty-seven cavalry are left to escort him to safety. This is very sad time for our arrogant hero Cao. His ambitious dream of united China is broken, at least for the time being.

Zhuge Liang, Kong Ming (181-234) was one of the greatest Chinese strategists of the Three Kingdoms period, as well as a statesman, astrologist, engineer, scholar, and inventor. Kong Ming was very loyal to Liu Bie, the leader of the Kingdom of Shu. He had never stopped fighting for his country. He might win some battles but he never won the war. He died in his battle camp at the age of fifty-three.

Kong Ming Capturing and Releasing the Barbarian King Meng Huo Seven Times

Meng Huo is the Barbarian King at the South Frontier of Shu. He is a great fighter and a good leader. China is torn among warlords, so he thinks he is entitled to have his fair share. In the month of May,he brings together a strong force of one hundred thousand soldiers and starts the invasion with the help of together a strong force of one hundred thousand soldiers and starts the invasion with the help of three Han Rebels,and the Grand Wardens: Yong Gui,and Zhu Bao and Grand Warden Gao Ding, and three Native-Chieftains,Marshal Jin Huan San Ji, Marshal Dong Cha Na, and Mashal A Hui Nan. One by one Kong defeats them all. At a treacherous and narrow pass, Kong plans an ambush. His soldiers capture Meng alive and deliver him in chains to the main camp. Meng refused to surrender. Kong aims at subduing his heart for long term peace. He releases him and Meng is glad to be free,but he will never give up fighting. He collects more than ten thousand cavalry from other tribes whilst waiting for the right moment to strike again. Two of the Marshals revolt against him. They bundle him up and hand him over to Kong Again Meng protests that this is not a fair fight. For the second time, Kong sets him free.

In the firey heat of the May Day sun, Kong orders his soldiers make camp with thatched roofs in the shade and rest, keeping away from the mid-day sun. This time, Meng sends his brother You to prey on Kong with a convoy of a hundred men carrying boxes of treasures, precious stones, ivory, gold and pearls as presents to Hong to show their gratitude. These men are tall and strong with yellow hair, purple beards, bare feet, bald head and wearing a gold earring. Their mission is when Meng attacks from out side they will provide assistance from inside. Kong returns their good will by treating them for a feast. They enjoyed drinking and eating but did not realise the food and wine are drugged. When Brother Meng comes to attack at the main camp, he finds no help but walks into a trap. Kong catches him the third time. Meng still refuses to surrender and Kong again lets him go.

The angry and desperate Meng sends for help from all the neighbouring tribes. A strong alliance of half a million men arrive. At first,the fighting seems quiet. Kong keeps his force inside the fort for days. He orders thirty thousand soldiers to cut down bamboos to make 1300 rafts. Then the fighting starts. Kong divides his force into two sections, one in front fighting and one to go sailing on rafts across the river to the back of the enemy camp. The enemies advance to the empty fort. By the time they retreat, their own camps are on fire. A smiling Kong appears in a small carriage in front, the angry chieftain with his thirty cavalry in a ferocious speed charge at him. Unfortunately Kong has prepared a deep ditch in front of them and they all fall into it. One by one these proud losers have to be lifted out. Our Chieftain has to face the humiliating defeat again instead of surrender, he challenges Kong to fight him in his native Home land. Kong agrees and let him go.

Meng's homeland is called Silver Pit Cave,and is surrounded by beautiful fertile farmland, salt wells and silver ore mines. On the hill stands many fine buildings and a family Shrine where they offer live human sacrifices (outsiders), for their Annual Sacred Ceremonial. These Barbarians are tough and cruel so are their women warriors; his wife, Lady Zhu Rong joins the fight, she is skilled in knife throwing. At the first round she captures two Shu generals. At the second round, she is caught by traps. She is escorted back to Meng's camp in exchange for the two generals.

In the meantime, the leader of Eight Outer Tribes rides on a white elephant comes to see Meng. The desperate Meng pleads for help from this leader, King of Mu Lu. Once again a fierce battle starts. Charging with his savage warriors, the King rides on top of his white elephant and employs the implacable witchcraft. He turns the battle field into a wild animals arena. Countless tigers, leopards, wolves and poisonous snakes jump on the soldiers. They win the first encounter but not for long. Kong is also a man of magic. At the second encounter, he sends out a herd of fiery gigantic monsters. Within minutes, he wins the battle, and the sorceries King is killed and,Meng's nest, the Silver Pit Cave is occupied by Kong. Next day, Meng is bundled up by his wife and brother and pretends to surrender and ask for mercy. This act of pretentious is foiled by Kong in no time. Meng declares this would be the last fight and it will be a straight fight with no tricks. Kong takes him at his word and releases him for the sixth time.

On his way home, Meng seeks help from King Wu Tu Gu of Wu Ge Kingdom. It is situated at the South East, seven hundred miles from here. King Wu Tu Gu is ten feet tall, eating no grains and no corns but feeding on live snakes,and wild beasts, his scale-covered body is immune from arrows and knives. His soldiers wear a kind of specially treated armour. It is made of canes and with some secret formula of herbs and oil. It takes nearly a year to tailor the materials. The finished product is so tough that no weapons can penetrate and it can float in deep water and come out dry in shallow water. As the assault starts, Kong tells his generals that they must retreat to get away from the brunt of the attack. Then he lures them into a valley called Snake Coiling Valley. Kong orders the blockage at both ends of the valley. With torches, explosives and all kinds of fire lighters, he burns the whole thirty thousand Cane Armour Soldiers in the Snake Coiling Valley. There is no escape but to burn to death. The battle is won. In tears Kong sighs, "I do this for my country, but I will have to pay for it. It will shorten my life span!" This time,the Barbarian King is truly repentant He swears he will never rebel again. Ever since there was peace and friendship between the two countries.

Brief biography of Luo Guanzhong:

Luo Guanzhong, (1330-1400), a native of Taiyuan (Shanxi today), was a Chinese author attributed with writing *Romance of the Three Kingdoms* and editing *Water Margin*. Luo Guanzhong is confirmed to have lived in the end of Yuan Dynasty and early Ming Dynasty. His father was a silk merchant. He started school at the age of seven. When he was fourteen, his mother died. His father wanted him to learn to do business with him. He was not keen in doing business and with his father's consent, he went back to scool studying from a famous scholar. Starting from the year 1356, he worked as an adviser to a powerful warlord Zheung. In the year 1363, he left Zheung and started writing and editing. On his way home, he met Shi Nai An and became his disciple. They lived together and they edited and wrote together. Unfortunately, The Emperor was not amused at Shi Nai An and his Water Margin. Shi was thrown into prison for more than a year. All the time, in or out of prison, Luo stayed loyal to his teacher. He nursed him until his end came. He gave him a proper burial. Luo also tried to publish Water Margin for his teacher. But no one would dare to offend the authority. He spent all his time and his energy to edit and to write his books. In 1400, he fell ill and died in Hangzhou at the age of seventy.

Summary of Three Kingdoms

The Novel is about the power struggle of three warlords: Cao Cao of Wei Kingdom (154-220), Liu Bei of Shu Kingdom (221-263), and Sun Quan of Wu Kingdom (160-250). They try to take over a weak Central Sovereignty, the Late Han Dynasty, 180-280 AD. They fight many bloody sea and land battles and recruit numerous brave generals and wise advisers to assist them. The most famous adviser is Kong Ming and the greatest general is Lord Guan. Soldiers and people suffer tremendously during the Three Kingdoms Period. But at the end of the day, no one is strong enough to win. All three Leaders die before their dreams come true. The Sima Clans, nobles of Wei, subdue the

Three Kingdoms one by one. Eventually China is united by Sima Yan, the first Emperor Wu of Jin (265-420). At last China has 155 years of peace and unity under the Jin Dynasty.

War and Peace
The Great War Novel in the West-
By Leo Tolstoy, (late in life) Russia 1828-1910

War and Peace written by Leo Tolstoy, was first published between 1865 and 1869. The novel tells the story of the aristocratic families and the entanglements of their personal lives with the history of 1805–1813, during Napoleon's invasion of Russia.

Many of Tolstoy's characters in *War and Peace* were based on real-life people known to the author, Tolstoy himself. Nikolai Rostov and Maria Bolkonskaya were based on Tolstoy's own memories of his father and mother, while Natasha was modelled after Tolstoy's wife and sister-in-law. Pierre and Prince Andrei could be Tolstoy himself. The central character to *War and Peace* is Pierre Bezukhov who, upon receiving an unexpected inheritance, is suddenly burdened with the responsibilities and conflicts of a Russian nobleman. His former carefree behavior vanishes. He enters into marriage with Prince Kuragin's beautiful and immoral daughter Elena. Tolstoy vividly depicts the contrast between Napoleon and the Russian general Kutuzov, and in the clash of armies. Finally, Napoleon is defeated by the Cossacks.

War and Peace has a vast cast of 580 people, 1474 pages and 4 volumes. Romance of the Three Kingdoms also has a grand total of 800,000 words, nearly 120 chapters. and 4 volumes. Both were undoubtedly the gigantic giants of the world literature.

CHAPTER 12

Water Margin
4th Great Chinese Classical Novel- By Shi Nai An 14th Century

The Famous Outlaws Novel– Water Margin

Foreword

Water Margin was written in 14th Century AD, Ming Dynasty, by Shi Nai An 1296-1372. Some say it was either written or edited by Luo Guan Zhong, the author of The Three Kingdoms. For some political reason, Luo does not want to reveal his true identity. The novel is written about 108 outlaws around the year 1101-1125 AD. During the reign of Emperor Ren Zong of Northern Song,these people are driven from the lawful society to the outlaw-refuge of Water Margin,Liang Shan Bo,a mountain surrounded by lakes, rivers and boggy land. Some of these outlaws are cruel and evil, killers of their corrupted and wicked enemies as well as innocent women and children. There are three versions of Water Margin. The 71 chapters 'version is most popular,the outlaws accept amnesty and live law abidingly ever after. In the 100 chapters version, the outlaws fight for the Emperor and gain merits through their services. In the 120 long version, the outlaws do not surrender but continue to challenge the Imperial authority for another fifty chapters and most of these outlaws die under the executioners' blade.

In this novel,there is very little history but a mixture of legend and fiction. The author introduces the 108 characters one by one, all with a nickname and with either a long or short biography, telling us why and how they become outlaws. It has 36 major and 72 minor characters. The first and the last chapter give a very superstitious opening and an incredible conclusion with a typical strong Taoist influence. I shall introduce a summarize translation of these Chapters later.

We all hear about Robin Hood,the Lord of Sherwood Forest and his Merry-men. We are told that they are noble and happy outlaws who fight injustice. Our 108 Chinese Robin Hoods also rob the rich and fight against the corrupted authority but they are not merry at all,nearly all of them are bitter and cruel. Most of our 108 bandits share a common background of crime-committing and then flee to Water Martin for refuge and keep on committing more evil crimes. Many are thirst for vengeance,they kill in the name of justice but in truth is mainly out of personal grudges, some plunder a whole village and town and very often in their violent fury, they hurt and kill the innocent and helpless with no mercy, similar to the horror of ethnic cleansing of our time. They act according to their gangsters' code of conduct and take the laws in their own hands. These outlaws are fierce, tough,cruel and skilful fighters. They kill, they rob, they plunder and they call themselves good man of Water Margin.

Everyone of them has a Celestial Star Title given by Heaven and Earth This absolute nonsense is unacceptable except for the ignorance and the underworld. Shi uses the most skilful dramatic effect and the superb cunning political trick to promote his Evil Outlaws (at least 50% of the 108 are really evils). He says it is Heaven's Will!

Some of these horrible outlaws are even cannibals, a well known Dark Inn at the Cross Road Slop making meat buns from human flesh. A horribly cruel outlaw, Li Kui, the Killer Star of Heaven, has a shocking habit of feasting and barbecuing on the flesh of his victims, slicing piece by piece from the body and climbs. In some occasion, he cuts open the chest and takes out the heart and liver to devour with hot wine. An extremely cruel and evil deed of all is the murdering of a healthy happy two years old son of the County Official. All because they want to recruit the child-minder to join them at Water Margin. Whenever they want to recruit somebody, they will use the dirtiest and cruellest tricks to force the poor victim to yield.

Many of these criminals are barbaric and beastly. Some are sick psychics and senseless monsters. They fight injustice with hellish vengeance. They are ten folds worse than injustice. Water Margin is a book of Killing, Horror and Cruelty. Many episodes are so very disgusting and cruel that no wonder the author does not want to reveal his true identity. No one in his right mind would be proud to be the writer of such a cruel and violent book, soaked with blood, nor would one enjoy reading such barbarity and sufferings with the heads rolling and the weak screaming. No wonder in over centuries,this book is considered to be the Encyclopaedia of the Under-world (Criminals). Of course It would be praised and approved by the Dark Force. To the law abiding citizen, we are perplexed and anguished! We do not know how Water Margin can be considered as one of the 4 Great Chinese Novels! I would like to point out to my readers that this is indeed one of the bloodiest and wickedest novels in Chinese Classical Literature. In early Ming Dynasty, Shi Nai An was imprisoned for two years and the book was banned by the First Emperor who was a far-sighted Emperor indeed.

3 Excerpts + Summaries from Water Margin

1. Chapter 1 and Chapter 71 108 Demons
2. Chapter 23 The Tiger Killer

3. Chapter 27,48, 49 Three Tigresses
4. Chapter 18-71 The Ringleader

Chapter 1 Marshal Hung Releasing the Demons

During the Five Dynasties (907-960) China falls into the hand of Warlords. In the year 960, Emperor Tai Zu unites China and establishes the Song Dynasty. People of China enjoy a long period of peace and prosperity under several succession of the Throne. Unfortunately, in the Reign of Song Ren Zong, a terrible plague sweep over China. People die in millions. In an urgent meeting, The Emperor and his Ministers decide to implement many urgent policies to alleviate the suffering of the people. One of these policies is to send for a reverend high priest to come to the Capital, Kaifeng, to perform a Heavenly Grand Mass, pleading to Heaven and God for help and for Mercy.

Zhang Tin See was the famous Wudang Taoist during the late years of the Yuan Dynasty and the beginning years of the Ming Dynasty. He was tall and strong. People believed that he had supernatural power. He could live without a meal for two or three months. He had written many books on medicine, but was also good in martial art.

The Emperor orders his Commandant-in-Chief, Marshal Hung Sheung to take the Imperial Decree to Superior Priest Zhang in Dragon and Tiger Mountain, Guang Xi Province. It is a very pressing and important case. Within days he reaches the Grand Taoist Temple Clear Palace. The Local officials and the priests give him a honourable reception. The Reverend Priest lives in a little hut at the top of the mountain. The Head Priest in charge advises Hong to climb up the mountain to show his great respect. Hung follows the advice. Dressed in cotton clothes, carrying the Decree at his back and holding incense in his hand, he climbs this treacherous path,encountering fierce tigers and poisonous snakes. At last his zealous devotion and arduous effort is rewarded. Half way to the peak, he meets a young cowherd and receives a message from the boy that Zhang Tian Shi is on his way to the Capital already!

Now mission accomplished, Hong is relaxed and pleased. His hosts entertain him with a lavish vegetable-banquet. Next morning after a good breakfast,the priests show him the scenic spots and the beautiful and glamorous temples around the Palace. When they come to a isolated building with the unusual red walls and two big red front doors. They sense the eerie atmosphere about the place. The doors are heavily chained with layers and layers of sealed labels mottled with ancient coded scriptures. At once the Taoist Priests advised him to leave. However our marshal is a brave and curious warrior. He insists on entering the place. As they walk inside into an empty Dark Grand Hall, lighted by twenty torches, they find in the middle of the Hall a 8 foot stone Plaque with mysterious ciphered scripture setting at the back of a Stone Tortoise. At the back of the Plaque, is written four big Characters, "Hung comes, then open!". Hung is bumptious and jubilant. He feels he is destined by Heaven to do the job. But when the plaque is lifted,black smoke accompanied by piercing thundering sound and glaring fleshing light, rushes out from the bottomless hole,shooting into the sky as dark clouds and dispersing to all directions. Everyone screams frightfully and runs for cover. Th eMarshal also trembles with fear and turns pale. Finally he realises he has released 108 demons (all turn outlaws) from captivity. The Chief Priest tells him, "These are the 36 Celestial Heaven Stars,72 Celestial Earth Stars. These are evil beings. Now they are out, the people of China will suffer."

Chapter 23 Wu Song the Tiger Slayer

The most famous outlaw in Water Margin is the Tiger Slayer, Wu Song His nickname is Vagabond Monk. Shih and the storytellers tend to over-praised him and depict a larger- than -life story about this Tiger Killing. They have created a superhuman. Wu Song becomes the most popular legendary symbol of strength and courage in Water Margin. Shih has written more than 10 chapters about this bitter and bloodthirsty outlaw and he also tells us how Wu kills people in the most horrible fashion. Wu Song not only kills beast but slaughters women and children mercilessly. You can believe that he has killed a tiger, if you want to. Even so, he does not do it with a noble motive not for the community, but for self-defence only! This is the most successful plot of Water Margin. People worship him for his mighty strength and extraordinary courage. Later obsessed with vengeance, he turns into a horrible senseless killer. No righteous human being should agree with those bloody slaughtering scene of the defenceless weak people. Yet,people are blind not to condemn his cruel killing of the innocent people. In the Celestial chart, his title is The Damage Star of Heaven. If one can murder 9 people all at one go, of course he is doing great damage to the community and is a evil damager. I am going to present this controversial character for you to judge him yourself.

Wu Song, a quarrelsome and drunken youth, is the native of Shan Dong Province, County Qing He. He is good looking,mighty and strong and with bad temper while his only elder brother is a four foot dwarf, repulsive looking but kind and timid. During a drunken fight,by mistake, Wu thinks he has killed a district Technician. He flees and hides. After nearly two years, he finds out this man is still alive. At present, he is tired of being a fugitive and wants to return home to see his dear brother. On his way back,he stops in an inn with a big Signboard over the door,"Three Cups Wine, No Crossing the Mountain Ridge!" The innkeeper explains to Wu that the wine has a very delicate flavour but is extremely strong. The locals call it 'Collapse By the Door' Usually, the innkeeper only serves the customer three cups. But Wu insists to have cup after cup or else he would smash the whole room and threaten to turn the place up side down. He drinks eighteen cups. Again ignores the innkeepers friendly warning of great danger ahead, he takes up his cudgel and sets off to Jing Yang Mount.

Now, he has come to Yang Gu, the District next to his home County with the King Yang Mount in between. Wu knows the place well. He has crossed Jing Yang Mount more than twenty times. It happened that this time,there is a ferocious tiger terrorising travellers. It comes out in the evening and has already killed thirty people and wounded many. The Local Authority issues big warning Killer Tiger Posters along the mountain path and on the ruined temple site. Finally, Wu realises the potential danger ahead. He chooses to go on rather than turn back to face the humiliation and scorn that he might get from the innkeeper.

The Autumn Day is getting shorter and darker. Half way to the Ridge, Wu decides to sleep on a smooth moss – covered rock. Just then he hears a loud roar from behind the tree. A huge tiger springs out and go straight to the kill. Wu manages to slip to the side. This ravenous beast tries the second time. This time Wu meets the tiger with his cudgel but he hits the tree instead of the tiger. At once, he throws away the broken cudgel and seizes the tiger by the neck with his mighty strength, forcing it to the ground, pinning its head to the earth,kicking it in the eyes, pressing its nose to the soil, holding the head skin of the tiger with his right hand and raining powerful blows with his left fist. The beast roars with pain. Blood sprout out from its eyes, nose and mouth. Wu picks up the broken cudgel and finishes the tiger off in his legendary tale.

Covered with blood and over-drained of his energy with killing the tiger, Wu wants to leave the mountain as quick as he can. Within a short distance, he meets two tigers. To his great relief, these are fake tigers accompanying by a group of hunters who are ordered by the magistrate to capture this man-eater dead or alive. Wu shows them the dead tiger and tells them he has done the impossible job for them. The hunters, the people of the county, the officials and the magistrate all salute him. They put this Tiger-killer in a sedan chair garlanded with red flowers and silk stripes, carried by four men and follows by the dead tiger also carried by four men. All the people of the county gather around the Office of the Magistrate to see the dead tiger and to cheer the bare hand tiger killer. He is awarded a large sum of money but he gives it away to the hunters who have suffered and tortured for not being able to capture this beast. It is a very happy and proud day for Wu! The Magistrate is greatly impressed by Wu's generosity, bravery and nobility. He appoints him to be the Head Constable of the police force. Day after day he dines and wines with the wealthy families as a Famous Celebrity.

One day he meets his beloved brother Big Man Wu, the peddler, in town and finds out he has married a pretty young maid, named Pan Jin Lian and they also live in Yan Gu. She hardly believes this tall and handsome hero is the blood brother of her ugly dwarf-husband.

She even tries to seduce him but in vain. Later with the help of her friend Wang Po, and her lover Xi Men Qing, a rich sex maniac, they poison Big brother Wu and then foully murder him. When Wu finds out his brother's tragic death, at first he goes to the authority and ask for justice. Xi Men is notorious but a very rich man. He bribes the corrupted officials high and low to get him out of trouble. They all advise Wu to drop the case.

Out of rage, frustration and grievance, Wu takes the law in his own hand, He does it in a big dramatic style. In his deceased brother's humble house, he orders two of his soldiers to prepare a small banquet for his neighbours and witness, decorates the small altar of big brother Wu with flowers, fruits, sacrificial food, incense, jolt sticks and wine. He orders two soldiers guard the front doors and two guard the back door. Frightened neighbours and unwilling observers are forced by Wu to come to his house as his witness. He forces out a detailed confession from his sister-in-law and her friend Wang Po. It is written down in black and white by one of the neighbours. Without hesitation, Wu cuts open the chest of Pan and scoop out her heart, lung etc., and then cuts off her head. That is not all. Wu finds Xi Men Qing and cuts off his head too. Now holding two heads, Wu turns himself in to the District Governor and also hand in Wang Po and the four witnesses. Wang Po is sentenced to death. As for Wu, he has committed a serious crime of passion. The Governor, in view of his heroic past, only sentences him to be exiled to County Meng, 2000 miles away and as all criminals have to go through, his face is tattooed with a special mark, the gold seal. No matter where he goes, people will recognise his criminal status.

Up to now Wu is only a fierce but decent convict. Until one day, in his new detention-centre, he gets involved with gangsters fighting with the Underworld over profit obtained from the gambling houses and brothels. Here is one of the most evil killing scenes. At first he kills four wicked men, send by their masters, Commander Zhang, Sheriff Zhang and Gate God Jiang. This is a bloody fight but for W it is self defence. Our hero is provoked and is furious. With his mighty strength and vigorously fighting skill, he chops them up and kicks them into the stream. Next, he goes to Army Commander Zhang's house and on his way in, he kills the rear- gate-guard and two kitchen maids. Up stairs, the three culprits are drinking and merry-making. Wu kicks his way in and within minutes their three heads roll on the floor of the dinning hall, That is not all, on his way out, he kills two more servants, Lady Zhang, a singer with two children and three more house-maids. After killing, eating, drinking and looting, Wu is quite satisfy with his evil and cruel slaughtering, Shamelessly, he dips blood with a piece of clothes from one of the dead body and writes on the wall:-

Killer of these People
Tiger Slayer Wu Song

After killing so many people, he flees, hides, listens to his bandit-friends and disguises himself as a travelling monk. They write him a letter to introduce him to join the Head Outlaws Ru Chee Sum and Yeung Chee in Two Dragons Mountain On his way, he kills two more people, an innocent boy and a evil priest. Wu stays in Two Dragons Mountain with his friends and becomes an outlaw not for long. Soon they join the main force, Water Margin and enjoy more raiding and killing for the rest of their days.

Brief Comment

In the beginning Wu is an innocent naughty boy. He drinks, he fights and he has a bad temper but he still has a good patch in his wayward nature. He loves his brother dearly, donates his Tiger Killing Award money to the Hunters Association, doing a good job as a Chief Constable. But once he starts cutting his enemies's head off and makes it a habit, he changes into a serial impulse killer. It gets into a horrible trend and he does not know when and where to stop. He becomes a dangerous menace. Out of the total 23 death, he beheads five people. He has great grievance and drowns himself in deep vengeance. We all condemn the corrupted officials and the injustice society but what he does is many times worse than injustice! Think of the screaming women and terrified children bath in blood! Think of the defenceless kitchen maids and the young priest being slashed down on the ground. Our author creates Wu Song, A Tiger and Men Killer. He successfully leads the storytellers plus many people to call Wu a Hero, despite of his gruesome cruelty to the innocent. Is this ignorance or stupidity? To me, Wu is sick and should be lock up for the rest of his life. He is a Sick Killer! (Water Margin is a Sick book!). Even in modern days, many scholars (so call scholars) still think Water Margin is a great Novel and Wu is a great hero. When I do the research on this Project I am amazed.

Chapter 27 48 49 Three Tigresses

Out of 108 bandits, three are women. Two are equally tough and cruel as men. One of these three women is the wife of the boss of a Black Inn. This inn serves the outlaws as an outpost, information Centre and a net work of spying. It is her job to drug her customers when she finds out they are not one of them. Then she dissects or cut up her victims to make meat buns etc. Both husband and wife are honoured and are positioned in the Chart of the Celestial of Mystery. Penalty Star of Earth is titled to the husband, Zhang Qing, nickname Gardener, Tough Star of Earth is the title given to the wife, 2nd Madam Sun, nickname Night Ogress. She is truly evil, the most evil demon of the three women.

The second woman outlaw in the novel is Gu Da Sao, nickname Tigress. She is a tough fighter. She helps her husband Sun Li, nickname Sick Man, to look after a restaurant and a gambling house at the back. One day Gu's two brothers get into serious trouble. They are law abiding hunters and after three days of perching up on the tree top,finally they killed a tiger. A malicious and greedy landowner, Old Master Mao, uses foul play to claim that the tiger is killed by his son Young Mao. He bribes the corrupted Authority to arrest the brothers and accused them of robbery and would be sentenced to death soon. When Sister Gu hears this terrible news, she gathers many friends and relatives and fight a bloody way to the prison to save the innocent hunters.

They kill the corrupted officials, the prison guards, Old Mao, his son and the whole family, old and young, men or women. Afterwards they raid the houses and gather cash and silver, bags of valuables and jewels, take all the handsome horses from the stable and burnt the Mao Family Village. After this massacre they go to join the outlaws of Water Margin. This is a good example of how ordinary people, such as the hunters, are driven from lawful society to the outlaw refuge. It also shows us that this massacre is not necessary. This is only a small scale village cleansing. Think of the large scale ones! How cruel ! How very cruel!

We all feel very sorry for this young and pretty lady, Hu San Niang. She comes from a wealthy family and she is a fierce fighter using two long knives. The Water Margin outlaws attack her village. She fights heroically but is captured by Lim Chong. It is a tragic outcome. These cruel outlaws lead by Li Kui kill everyone in the Hu Family Village. Her courageous brother Hu Long fights his way out and is the only survivor. Song Jiang takes special care of her and makes her his adopted sister. When the fighting is over, he does match-making. The poor girl is forced to marry a notorious womaniser, Wang Ying. Wang is greedy and ugly yet rather loyal to Water Margin. Hu comes to terms with her fate and becomes one of the outlaws, titled The Clever Celestial Star of Earth. Her family background is decent and wealthy. She is gentle and nice,a proper gentle lady, talented in martial arts. Song,the outlaw leader,has a special respect for her and treated her with distinctive favour. She is the only good lady among these evil –gangsters

Li Kui, a cruel cannibal and habitual killer, was one of the strongest amongst the 108 Liangshan bandits and also the cruelest. He is one of the 36 Heavenly Chieftains., nicknamed "The Black Whirlwind" or "Iron Ox"

Out of 108 bandits, Li Kui is the real horror and kills more people than any bandits in the whole Novel. He is cruel! He is crazy! He is very sick! He waves his Double Axe and chops people like chopping carrots and cucumbers. He is the Devil itself! A lively four year child is murdered by him.

Nowadays most of us have a good education or at least with some education. Still it is not easy to have an independent thought. Our thought and behaviour are more or less affected by media and politics. No wonder after a thousand years, there are still so many Chinese, mature adults and youngsters alike, wrongly lead by media and novels, blindfolded themselves to worship these brutal Killers. In the 21st century, we have no storytellers in the Market place and hardly any in the Supermarket but the novel (translated in English,French, Japanese, Germen.) is quite popular. Obviously, the colourful TV and the film maker produce Water Margin in a more influential way than the storytellers. Some only concern themselves in money -taking, not the morality of the masses. Media can manipulate people's thought and action. The Sub-culture of the Dark Force and Brutal Crimes should never be glorified nor should be encouraged. We should have a clear mind to face the crime and horror in the novel and call a spade a spade, never cosmetic ugly villain and criminals to handsome heroes. I do agree that it was very good of the first Emperor of Ming dynasty to ban the book and put the author in prison for two years.

Chapter 18—The Ring Leader Song Jiang

Song Jiang who works as a judge in the District Magistrate is the elder son of a small landowner. He always helps people in need and thus earns a nickname, Timely Rain. Some of his friends are criminals and fugitives. Eventually he gets involved in a big Theft- The Birthday Treasure which leads to a killing of a young woman, his kept girl. Now it is his turn to be a Fugitive and during his wayward encounters, he makes many bold friends, many from the Water Margin.

One night, as he is drunk, he commits a fatal imprudence, writing a rebellious poem against the Imperial Authority. A Clerk, Wang Wen Bing. reports this to the Prefecture Cai Jiu. It is these outlaws from Water Margin save him from the Execution Axe of the Authority. He does not mind to be a friend of the outlaws but never wants to be one. But in the Big Operation of Rescue, his bandit friends from Water Margin rescue him from the Executing platform, killing hundreds of soldiers and civilians. About fifty members of the Wang family, young and old. male and female, all have been slaughtered by these horrible gangsters. They raid and return their nest with bags and sacks of silver, jewels and valuable stuffs.

Now here is the Killing of No Return. Song has to join Liang Shan Bo Gangsters and eventually becomes their Number One Ring Leader.

From now on he plans, he raids, he plunders and gives the consent to allow his fellow – gangsters to cleanse an entire village or town. In the name of doing Justice, most of the time, these gangsters bring evil and disaster to people, ten times worse than Injustice. Of all the plundering and killing, the cruellest and senseless one is the city cleansing

In the historical record of Song Dynasty, there was a real bandit, Song Jiang. He was recorded as the leader of a bandit group in the 12th century, during the Song Dynasty. His group plundered and killed in the present-day provinces of Shandong and Henan, before surrendering to government troops. He featured as the hero-leader of the classic Chinese novel Water Margin, on Mount Liang. He was known as Timely Rain.

The Folklore Goddess of Nine Heaven, (Nuwa)is mythological character best known for reproducing people. To enforce absolute power and reverence from the gangsters, Song declares he meets the goddess of Nine Heaven in his dream. He says he is given a contract, written in three books. These sacred books will guide him how and what to do in future.

Song Jiang is real. Base on Chinese Historical Record, there is a bandit named Song Jiang in thirteenth century, Northern Sung Dynasty. He has 36 bold men with him, nesting in Water Margin, a Mountain in Shangtung Province, set in numerous small lakes and streams surrounded by mashes. Later on, the author arranges the Official Appearance of the Celestial Titles of these 108 outlaws in a stone-plaque. He tries to convince the reader that it is the will of Heaven for these bloody gangsters to plunder, to raid, to cheat, to murder and to slaughter. They declare they fight tyranny and injustice. In fact the inevitability of brutal murder and slaughter is the norm of the gangsters in this Novel. We should have a clear head to reject all the random killing. I have to admit that this novel is cleverly written. The description of the livelihood of the people in Ming society is interesting and minute; bring out 108 gangsters on to the stage one by one is a fantastic Novel with a foul Soul. It has successfully drawn the interest of millions readers and attracts their keen attentions over hundreds of years. A healthy society must have a healthy conscious to condemn such Dark Force.

Chapter 71 Names of the Heaven Stars and Earth Stars on the Plaque: *This is the last chapter concluded the 108 characters of the outlaws.*

In the mean time, the outlaws are quite pleased with their achievement. They build a Three Layers Grand Altar and invite many Taoist Priests to offer a splendour Mass for the living and the death. On the 7th day, at mid-night, a loud thunder, accompanying by blinding-lightening and a Roaring fire, an object is seen fallen down from Heaven and buried under the crack of the ground near the Altar in front of the big gathering of the outlaws. In tremendous fear and awe,they search what is in the crack. After digging three feet deep, they find a stone-plaque with a Chart of ancient scripture. Nobody can break the code. Among the priests, a Senior Priest comes forward. For generations his family keep an ancient holy book. He studies that book for years and gains the super natural power to break the Code. He tells them that by the side it says :-

Follow the Will of HeaveWe Serve
By Loyalty and VirtueWe Survive

Each of the outlaws has a title of a special Celestial Star, in a total of 36 Heaven Stars and 72 Earth Stars. The Ringleader of Water Margin is Song Jiang, nickname Timely Rain. He is at the top of the Chart, called The Supreme Star of Heaven. He is the Judge of the County Court. Unwillingly he gets involved with the Water Margin Out laws and eventually he becomes their Ring Leader. The writer tries to guide the simple minded masses to accept that these brutal outlaws and murderers. He says, "It is all Heaven's Will."

Liangshan County is a county in Shandong province, China. The area is the setting for the classic novel, the Water Margin. Mount Liang is a mountain in Liangshan County, Shandong province, China. It is well known as the nest of the 108 legendary Song Dynasty bandits of the classic Chinese novel Water Margin. Water Margin describes Mount Liangshan in majestic terms, imagining its peak to be a plateau ringed by high mountains and protected by six passes and eight fortresses, surrounded by marsh-land. Now a number of buildings have been erected to match descriptions given in Water Margin. The mountain now has a somewhat theme park for tourists.

Summary

In the Northern Sung Dynasty, 12th (13th ?) century, there was much corruption and injustice in China. By the Will of Heaven, 108 Celestial Demons were released into the community. One by one, each has gone through different adventures, most of them are brutal criminals, some are law abiding people but driven by corrupted authority to become outlaws, some are courageous officials yet framed and forced by the outlaws to become one of them, eventually all of them take refuge in Water Margin, a mountain in Shan Dong Province, surrounded by lakes, rivers and marshes. These 108 outlaws band together to fight evil with evil. They robbed, they plunder, they kill. Every now and then they even burn down the whole town and they slaughter the whole village. In the final chapter the Ringleader Sung Jiang, pledged, in the name of Heaven, to go straight.

Emperor Hongwu

The Emperor and the Author:

Emperor Hongwu was the founder of the Ming dynasty. He was a man of action, a bold and shrewd tactician, and a creative genius. Hongwu died in 1398 at the age of 69. When he read Water Margin, he was not amused. He found the book too treacherous, bloody and cruel. Many of the criminals were barbaric and rebellious. The Emperor was furious. Shi Nai An was thrown into prison by this able Emperor for two years and the book was banned by the Emperor who was a far-sighted Emperor indeed.

Shi Nai An, 1296-1372., was a classical Chinese author from Suzhou city, Jiangsu province. He came from a poor family and could only afford to go to a proper school at the later age of 13. He studied hard and eventually passed the three level imperial examinations. At the age of 36, he was appointed to be a district official. He was not happy at work and resigned at the age of 38. Then he started teaching and writing. He married twice. Water Margin was written in early Ming Dynasty by him. Luo Guan Zhong the author of The Three Kingdoms studied in his school and became his faithful disciple. Some say Water Margin was either written or edited by Luo Guan Zhong. After releasing from prison, Shi died shortly at the age of 76. His trusty disciple Luo Guan Zhong was with him all the time.

There is a saying in ancient China, "It is not advisable for young people to read Water Margin. It is not advisable for old People to read Three Kingdoms." It is simply because young people might get the bad influence from the criminal deeds from the Outlaws and could end up in, cruel and senseless fighting all day long. Three Kingdoms is treacherous. Old people should try to enjoy a peaceful, simple and happy life. Scheming or planning to harm other will bring no good to their health, physically and mentally.

Robin Hood – the English Folk Hero

Robin Hood is the archetypal English folk hero; a courteous, pious and swashbuckling outlaw of the mediæval era who, in modern versions of the legend, is famous for robbing the rich to feed the poor and fighting against injustice and tyranny. He operates with his "seven score" (140 strong) group of fellow outlaws, named the Merry Men. He and his band are usually associated with Sherwood Forest, Nottinghamshire. Our 108 Chinese outlaws, around the year 1101-1125 A. D, Song Dynasty, seek refuge of Water Margin, Liang Shan Bo, a mountain surrounded by lakes, rivers and boggy land

Sherwood Forest is a world famous country park surrounding the village of Edwinstowe in Nottinghamshire, England. Sherwood Forest is a popular tourist attraction and attracts 500,000 tourists annually, including many from around the world. It is home to Robin Hood and his Merry men. Little John is presumably a fictional character in the legend of Robin Hood. Usually, John is depicted as Robin's second-in-command of the Merry Men.

In some versions Robin Hood is said to have been a nobleman, the Earl of Loxley, who was deprived of his lands by greedy churchmen. In some tales he is the champion of the people, fighting against corrupt officials and the oppressive order that protects them. In others he is an arrogant and headstrong rebel.

The Death of the Folk Hero

In the chamber where this dying chieftain lay. The latter, according to the story in the ballad, makes the following request:
'Give me my bent bow in my hand,
And an arrow I'll let free,
And where that arrow is taken up,
There let my grave digged be.'

The Grave of Robin Hood

The bow being then put into his hands by Little John, Robin discharged it through the open casement, and the arrow alighted on a spot where, according to popular tradition, he was shortly afterwards buried at the age of 86. A stone, carved with a florid cross and an obliterated inscription, marks the place of scripture, and the whole aera has been in recent times surrounded by an enclosure, as shown in the accompanying engraving. This probably genuine memorial of Robin Hood, is situated on the extreme edge of Kirklees Park, not far from Huddersfield. The site which it occupies is bold and picturesque, commanding an extensive view of what was formerly forest land, and which still displays clumps of gnarled oaks.

(I am deeply indebtd to Mr. Mike Hillman and Mr. Robert Chamber, the authors, giving consent to use the image and to use the story related to Robin Hood.)

Religion and I

Foreword

My ancestral and traditional religious-value provides me with a fantastic playground. Many Taoists create the magical deities and provide many fantastic settings. I grew up in this colourful 'Fairy Tale Wonderland.' Confucius said, "Revere Heaven and Earth". This is a solemn motto of Confucianism. My father is a devoted Confucian. To my father, Heaven is God. As a child, with awe, I firmly believe that 'Heaven-God' is everywhere. With excitement, I always enjoy the Taoist's (my mother's) many fun gods. In my childhood, I believe as long as I am obedient and God Fear, I will live a happy life.

I was educated in Protestant and Catholic schools. I was taught the 10 commandments and the Sermon on the Mount. It is quite easy to understand. I learned these teachings and scored in my mind for the rest of my life. I also learned to confess my sin with repentance. Then I would be forgiven and free from most troubles and worries. I live in a Christian country. From birth to death, Christian or no Christian, the Church pays a important part in our life. I am never baptised. My husband is a Catholic. We married in Church and so were my children. My in-laws were buried with the Catholic church service. We spent a few hours in Church and that was it. It was solemn and short. My parents were too traditional. They wanted a traditional funeral service which lasted for 49 days. It was a very colourful ritual; with dancing, chanting and offering high masses by different groups of monks and nuns to the death. How fascinating!

I keep Buddhism to one little chant, "Namo Amitabba Buddha." This is the only basic concept I know about Buddhism. To me, 'Amitabba' is the same one as the 'All Mighty God' in the Bible; Allah in The Holy Qur'an and my father's Heaven God, all but with a different name. I consider myself more than lucky to be blessed by these glorious religions

Greatest Religion of Mankind-Christianity

SERMON ON THE MOUNT

Jesus came to Mount Zion, meeting the multitudes. Jesus went up on the mountain, and when He was seated, His disciples came to Him. Then He opened His mouth and taught them, saying:

1. "Blessed are the poor in spirit,
   For theirs is the kingdom of heaven.

2. Blessed are those who mourn,
   For they shall be comforted.

3. Blessed are the meek,
   For they shall inherit the earth.

4. Blessed are those who hunger and thirst for righteousness,
   For they shall be filled.

5. Blessed are the merciful,
   For they shall obtain mercy.

6. Blessed are the pure in heart,
   For they shall see God.

7. Blessed are the peacemakers,
   For they shall be called sons of God.

8. Blessed are those who are persecuted for righteousness' sake,
   For theirs is the kingdom of heaven.

Moses with the Ten commandments
by Rembrandt (1659)

The Ten Commandments are a set of Biblical principles relating to ethics and worship. Different groups follow slightly different traditions for interpreting and numbering them. When Moses came down from the mountain with the Ten Commandments, he saw his people worshipped the golden calf. In great wrath, he cast the tablets out of his hands, and broke them beneath. God is merciful. He gives the tablets to Moses once more, the second time.

10 Commandments

1. I am the Lord your God, you shall have no other gods before me.
2. You shall not make for yourself an idol.
3. You shall not make wrongful use of the name of your God.
4. Remember the Sabbath and keep it holy.
5. Honour your father and mother.
6. You shall not murder.
7. You shall not commit adultery.
8. You shall not bear false witness against your neighbour.
9. You shall not covet your neighbour's wife.
10. You shall not covet your neighbour's goods.

Islam and I

I know very little about Islam but. I shall never forget my field day in the Mosque. The Holy Qur'an is one of the most beautiful holy books on top of my desk. The front and the back hard cover is decorated in bright gold colour pattern and so are the words, all embedded in the luxurious dark green back ground

When I was in Edmonton, I helped out as an assistant teacher in the Immigrant Centre once a week. One of my students was my neighbour. We became friends. One day she invited me to her mosque. She showed me round the nursery and the kitchen. With awe and respect, I enjoyed this visit thoroughly. Better still, before the day was over, a senior member gave me a brand new beautiful Qur'an.

(Full name-The Meaning of The Holy Qur'an). I remembered we were sitting and talking merrily. As the Qur'an is big and heavy, I put it on the floor. This kind lady came over immediately. With a smile in her face, she said, "We always treat the Holy Book with great respect. Do you think we should pick it up from the floor.?" From then on, wherever I go, I make sure my Holy Book is properly placed.

Up to now, I have read 736 out of 1758 pages in my beautiful Holy Qur'an. When I finish doing my book project, I shall speed up my reading. It is a promise and I will not forget it!

'The meaning of The Holy Qur'an'

The meaning of The Holy Qur'an' is the monumental work of Abdullah Yusuf Ali, 14 April 1872—10 December 1953. He was a Indian Islamic scholar who translated the Qur'an into English. His translation of the Qur'an is one of the most widely-known and used in the English-speaking world. To me, these few lines have tremendous impact on my religious belief. Below is from the very first page of my Holy Qur'an.

In the Name of Allah,
The Compassionate, the Merciful,
Praise be to Allah, Lord of the Universe,
And Peace and Prayers be upon
His Final Prophet and Messenger.

Ancient Chinese Religion— Three in One

1. Taoism (Chinese Folk Religion) Founder—Laotze 604-521 BC

2. Confucianism Founder Confucius 551-479 BC

3. Buddhism Founder Gautama Buddha 6th century BC

Chinese Religion

Strictly speaking Chinese Religion in China is the combination of three religions in one. It has been practiced alongside Buddhism, Confucianism, Taoism and ancestor worship (Folk Religion) by Chinese people throughout the world including Mainland China and Taiwan, Singapore and Overseas Chinese Communities. It is estimated that there are at least 800 million followers to Chinese folk religion worldwide. It is one of the major religious traditions in the world.

Chinese folk religion includes the veneration of the sun, the moon, the earth, the heaven, and various stars, as well as animals. The Chinese dragon is one of the key religious icons in these beliefs. If you ever enter my study, you will find a huge white toy monkey sitting on top of my book shelf. My mother once told me that the Monkey King is my Godfather who saved me from my high fever. It sounds silly. But subconsciously, I pay special respect to this big fluffy Monkey King. It perches high in the corner, looking down at me, sharing my dreams. As long as I live, I will revere it and to me, this is the power of folk religion.

Chinese Folk Religion has a long list of gods and goddesses

I grew up among numerous gods and goddess as well as "saints," and immortals. I choose a few well-known names here to represent some commonly worshipped deities. In our beautiful 'Fairy Tales' land, the deities are all amazingly powerful, full of magic and charm. We believe that they are kind and just. 'Help the good and weak but punish the villain and evil' is their duty.

These are a few of the popular Chinese Folk deities:

1. Cai Shen, God of Wealth who oversees the gaining and distribution of wealth, often appears at the Chinese New Year Celebration and hand out 'Lucky Red Packet.' He wears a long red robe and a black long beard in his smiling face.
2. Zao Shen, God of Kitchen, is in the kitchen. He reports to heaven on the behave of the family of the house once a year at Chinese New Year. Before he goes to see the Jade Emperor in heaven, he is given a little banquet as a small bribe in exchange for a good report.
3. Tu Di Gong, the "God of the earth", somewhat like our local councillor, who protects a local place, and whose office may be found in roadside shrine. He is the god protecting local people from monsters and he is also the god guarding wealth, minerals and buried treasure.
4. Emperor Guan is a figure of courage and righteousness. He is respected as an example of loyalty and virtue. In Hong Kong all the police stations have a special place to revere him. If you look carefully in Chinatown, Liverpool, you will find in some restaurants, our Emperor Guan standing in a quiet corner, protecting the establishment and bringing them good business.
5. The Eight Immortals are important literary and artistic figures who were deified after death. They are witty and humane. Most of them are said to have been born in the Tang Dynasty or Song Dynasty. They are revered in the Chinese folk religion culture. People like them because this gang of eight has no class, no sex and

no age barrier at all. It includes the old and young, rich and poor, male and female. Before they became deities, they were ordinary mortals.

Kannon statue in Daienin Mt. Koya, Japan

6. Guanyin, the Goddess of Mercy, is an extremely popular Goddess in Chinese folk belief and is worshiped in Chinese communities throughout the world. She is generally regarded by many as the Goddess of unconditional love, compassion and mercy. In recent years there have been claims of her being the protector of not just mainly to women and children but as well as to air travelers. Due to her symbolizing compassion, Guanyin is associated with vegetarianism. Guanyin is revered in the general Chinese population by Taoists and Buddhists. Some Buddhist schools refer to Guanyin both as male and female interchangeably. To the Chinese Taoists, Guanyin is an Immortal. Sometimes she appears with a thousand arms and often depicts as a tall beautiful lady wearing a long white robe or sitting on top of a lotus-seat. In short she is the most popular immortal and the highest in Chinese folk religion. If I remember correctly, Guanyin (he) is in the 2nd (out of eight ranks) highest rank of the Buddha's Pure Land.

Buddhism and I

This is a very short article about Buddhism and I. To me Buddhism is too deep and too complicated. One of my good friends in Edmonton is a nun. After spending hours after hours with me, she know that I will never be a philosophical Buddhist because I am simple, shallow and forgetful. Nevertheless, by chance, I learnt how to say a magnificent little chant and I was told about the meaning of this chant by her. One day if you see me saying nothing but smiling quietly, you know that I might be chanting. This very little chant gives me peace and relief especially when I am in trouble. I like this Chant very much. My friend told me that repetitive chanting of this little chant with utmost faith and a sincere vow is the way to achieve happiness in the Pure Land, West Paradise. The deep philosophical value is totally beyond my understanding. But it reminds me of the God in the Holy Bible. Do you think we are talking about the same God in the same Paradise?

Meaning of the Chant—"Namo Amituofo"

Namo means to pay highest homage and greatest respect.

Amituofo is the name of the Supreme Buddha of the boundless light, most superior and compassionate, The Buddha of Infinity.

One day if you see me saying nothing but smiling quietly, you know that I might be chanting. This very little chant gives me peace and relief especially when I am in trouble. I am good in getting into trouble. I like and I need this little Chant very much indeed. My friend told me that repetitive chanting of this little chant with utmost faith and a sincere vow is one of the ways to achieve happiness in the Pure Land, West Paradise. The deep philosophical value is totally beyond my understanding. But it reminds me of the God in the Holy Bible. Do you think we are talking about the same God in the same Paradise?

MY WARDS AND I
(48 HOURS IN THE DARK TUNNEL)

Forty four years ago, as a teacher, I left Hong Kong for Liverpool, to be nanny to two young babies,- my 16 month son, and newly born daughter. My husband gave up his job as a civil servant in Hong Kong and took up a post as a restaurant manager in UK This was a big change, but it did not take me long to adapt to my new role.

Ten years quickly passed. My husband took us back to Hon Kong on a short Duty Call to visit our aging parents. The children were very happy and excited; they were both healthy and well-mannered.

This was my family's best period. All the people we knew, family and friends, gave us the best and warmest receptions, sight-seeing tours every day and marvellous dinner parties every night. We felt happy and proud when sharing the experiences of our humble lives abroad with them. The ten years self-imposed exile had its own good rewards.

1973 was a very uncertain year in Hong Kong. Many families wished to send their children to boarding schools in UK, and pleaded to me to be their children's guardian in Liverpool. I have a reputation as a strict teacher, Assistant Prefect of Studies in a school of 3000 students.

Those parents all knew that I believed in caring and in sharing as well as discipline.

My husband was not a fighter but very industrious, honest and kind, a person of integrity. For those ten long years he worked without respite; no weekends off and holidays were unknown. The duties of a restaurant manager are many,- waiter, barman, cashier, buyer, bouncer, and whatever, if and when necessary. He enjoyed the good income, but not the long hours. There was not much choice for us. He soldiered on and was very careful with his hard-earned money. He invested carefully in property in Hong Kong for retirement and contingencies. He had promised my father to take us all back to Hong Kong when he had gathered enough money. Sadly, my father passed away the following year.

At weekends the house was crowded with many teenagers. They were all well-behaved and achieving well in school. One of the boys went to the Medical School at Liverpool University. Others wanted to follow, but as I was their guardian, I had to ensure their futures were planned carefully and correctly. In the end there were four successful dentists in Liverpool, one medical doctor, two senior managers, three managing directors of large companies, and an engineer.

Their success owed much to their parents. In one case, the parents, both teachers, sold their home to pay university fees for their two sons This impressed me very much. I paid special attention to these boys. Now the mother has passed away, and the father, a healthy near ninety years old man, lives in a good retirement home, and plays Tai Chi every day. He was the Grand Master who started a branch of Tai Chi in Liverpool.

Some of my wards still keep in touch. A few years ago, I attended a funeral in Hong Kong, and I stayed in one family home in Bentham Road, just across the road from HKU. I was glad and grateful if not overwhelmed, and I expressed this to my host, then a senior manager. She smiled and said, 'I always remember you as my Liverpool mum.' What a complement!

In Liverpool town centre there was once a very nice restaurant. I was invited by my best friend, Mr. Soo, one of the owners, to have a meal, and like love at first sight, it became my dream restaurant. At that time, we were looking for business, specially for restaurant. Mr. Soo wanted to buy the other two partners out. He needed financial backing, so he naturally turned to us to offer a partnership. My husband was experienced and successful in this trade. Happily but naively I included my sister and her husband, the parents of three of my wards. They were newly arrived immigrants from Hong Kong, and they knew I would give them every help to settle in this new land. They were industrious and had accumulated a good fortune, but were too young to retire. I was overjoyed to be able to welcome them and help them.

Anyone could see that I was excessively enthusiastic, and this annoyed my children. But I saw it as a great privilege and God's blessing. Many of us, ladies, jokingly called ourselves that we were overseas orphans, with no relatives around us at all. My sister was my own flesh and blood! I was no longer an orphan! When my sister declared that she came to Liverpool with a whole family, 5 Leungs because of me, I was in heaven!

I was very happy to help these new arrivals to find a large and beautiful house, to buy good investment property, and to introduce them to my best friend to negotiate the restaurant together. We thought then that the business hunting was over. But after a long wait, I discovered devious activity in the background; the restaurant was gone. My sister had betrayed us! Mr. Soo needed my sister's money to buy out the other partners, but did not want to share further. My husband was too good for them. I also discovered that these 'Father and Son team' together with my sister, my own flesh and blood, used me, deceived me and then left me in the Dark Tunnel. What a shameless conspiracy! My sister is rich, and she knew her jobless husband would not get a better chance than this. She used all kinds of tricks, cunningly and shamelessly to achieve their conspiracy. Deceitfully and wily, they put us in the dark. This treacherous gang succeeded.

My discovery of this betrayal left me devastated. I had a few sharp and short black outs but I told no body. The family thought it was all my fault to allow this pack of wolves to come to our home and harm us. Reluctantly, my husband accepted a well-paid job in Hong Kong. In 1976, many people tried to leave HK. It seemed ridiculous for us to move the family back to the colony. I like Liverpool. We were a well-regarded and happy family. Now I had to plan boarding schools and a guardian for the children. I was extremely depressed, hopelessly trapped, confused, shattered, angry, disappointed and sad. I was drained with sorrow and did not know how to fight these greedy schemers and deceitful traitors.

I found myself trapped in a dark tunnel; days later I was told I had had a nervous breakdown for 48 hours. This was a mysterious experience for me, but far more devastating for the young children and the family. My husband took the fastest flight home. When in my dark tunnel, I felt tired and lonely. Then I saw a dim light. A voice said softly, 'Be calm, be brave, think of the family and your dream. Right is Might! Go back to fight.' I followed that light and walked out of the tunnel, to find my husband holding my hand, the children smiling, and the doctor giving me one more injection.

The ordeal was over, but with a sting in the tail. I had to take medication for the rest of my life. After the ordeal, I lost the trust of my children. That is the greatest loss.

Chinatown in Liverpool is the same as any small community anywhere. Gossip and tittle-tattle are people's norm. Before my husband retired and went to Canada, I worked as a community worker in Pagoda for three years and as a shop manageress in the Post Office for 6 years. People are kind and show no discrimination. When I retired and started my colossal book project, my small team of advisors and helpers gave me support and encouragement. The Voice in the Tunnel is my compass!

Regardless of the great turmoil, my wards still showed respect in me. I remembered many years ago, I had to give a young woman a

Special One–to- One -Talk. Strictly speaking, she was no longer my ward. She gained a professional degree with a good income but got a reputation being greedy and selfish. When she becomes overboard with her folly, I gave her a friendly and very serious talk for one whole hour. She was in tears and seemed repentant.   Now as a regular church goer in Woolton, she might have turned a new leaf.

In 1997, I started to put my dream book to paper, then to computer. I also like people to be very careful of the very dark side of human nature, selfishness and greed.   No cover-up and no exaggerations,   I unreservedly, present my '48 Hours in the Dark Tunnel' to you.

Please remember this saying:-
In God I Trust